SMART INSTANT POT COOKBOOK

Healthy And Foolproof Instant Pot Recipes for Smart People And Everyday Cooking with Beginners Guide.

BY

Michael Francis

ISBN: 978-1-952504-55-6

COPYRIGHT © 2020 by Michael Francis

All rights reserved. This book is copyright protected and it's for personal use only. Without the prior written permission of the publisher, no part of this publication should be reproduced, distributed, or transmitted in any form or by any means, including photocopying, recording, or other electronic or mechanical methods.

This publication is sold with the idea that the publisher is not required to render accounting, officially permitted, or otherwise qualified services. If advice is required, it is necessary to seek the services of a legal or professional, a practiced individual in the profession. This document is geared towards providing substantial and reliable information in regards to the topics covered.

DISCLAIMER

The information written in this book is for educational and entertainment purposes only. Strenuous efforts have been made to provide accurate, up to date and reliable complete information. The information in this book is true and complete to the best of our knowledge. All recommendation are made without guarantee on the part of the author and publisher.

Neither the publisher nor the author takes any responsibility for any possible consequences of reading or enjoying the recipes in this book. The author and publisher disclaim any liability in connection with the use of information contained in this book. Under no circumstance will any legal responsibility or blame be apportioned against the author or publisher for any reparation, damages, or monetary loss due to the information herein, either directly or indirectly.

Table of Contents

INTRODUCTION 8

What is an Instant Pot? 9

Benefits of Cooking with Your Instant Pot 10

Making Sense of Your Instant Pot Buttons 11

Instant Pot Accessories (Must-Have Tools) 14

How to Clean Your Instant Pot (Cleaning Tips) 16

Instant Pot FAQ – Frequently Asked Questions 18

    Before Purchasing Instant Pot 18

    After Purchasing Instant Pot 19

Troubleshooting Tips 20

BREAKFAST 22

    Bacon and Egg Risotto 22

    Strawberry Trail Mix Oatmeal 23

    Breakfast Hash 24

    Spanish Chorizo & Potato Hash 25

    Apple Bread with Salted Caramel Icing 26

    French Toast Casserole 27

    Breakfast Cobbler 28

    Ham & Egg Casserole 29

    Quinoa Blueberry Breakfast Bowl 30

    Western Omelets Quiche 31

    Cinnamon Brown Rice Pudding 32

    Breakfast Burrito Casserole 33

SOUPS & STEWS 34

    Red Pepper Tomato Soup 34

    Spanish Infused Chicken Stew 36

Italian Wedding Soup 37

Andouille Sausage Stew 38

Hearty Broccoli Soup 39

Italian Beef Stew 41

White Bean Parmesan Soup 42

Spicy Ethiopian Stew 43

Creamy Thai Coconut Chicken Soup 44

Tomato Chick Pea Soup 45

Beef & Butternut Squash Stew 46

Cuban Shredded Beef Stew 48

Creamed Fennel and Cauliflower Soup 50

Hearty Beef Stew 51

CHICKEN 52

Honey Teriyaki Chicken 52

BBQ Chicken Sliders 54

Teriyaki Rice with Chicken & Vegetables 55

Chicken Paprika 57

Faux-Tisserie Chicken 58

Cajun Chicken and Rice 60

Chicken Pho 62

Butter Chicken 64

Spicy Honey Chicken 65

Salsa Chicken Tacos 66

FISH & SEAFOODS 67

Easy Coconut Red Curry Shrimp 67

Steamed Alaskan Crab Legs 69

10-Minute Instant Pot Salmon 70

Shrimp and Lentil Stew 71

Bang Bang Shrimp Pasta 72

Creamy Chipotle Shrimp Soup 73

Alaskan Cod with Fennel, Olives and Potatoes... 74

Lemon Pepper Salmon 76

Fish and Corn Chowder 77

Lobster Bisque 78

TURKEY... 79

Turkey Meatball & Ditalini Soup 79

Pumpkin Turkey Chile Mole 81

Italian Turkey Stuffed Sweet Potatoes 83

Turkey Chili 84

Turkey Vegetable Lasagna Soup.. 86

Turkey-Stuffed Peppers 88

Turkey Taco Pasta 89

Turkey & Pumpkin Chili 90

BEEF... 92

Beef Ragu... 92

Beef Bourguignon 94

BBQ Beef Short Ribs.. 96

Beef Chili.. 98

Vietnamese Beef Brisket Tacos 99

Italian Tomato Meatballs 101

Chunky Beef, Cabbage & Tomato Soup.. 102

Beef Picadillo 103

Beef & Chorizo Chili 104

Korean Ground Beef Bulgogi... 105

PORK 106
- Savory Pork Burrito Bowls 106
- Smoked Pulled Pork 107
- Pork Vindaloo 108
- Mexican Pulled Pork 110
- Pork Barbecue Sandwiches 111
- Creamy Mushroom Sauce Pork 112
- Salsa Pork Chops 113
- Mississippi Pork Sandwiches 114
- Crispy Pork Carnitas 116

VEGAN & VEGETARIAN 117
- Broccoli Soup with Gremolata 117
- Vegetables En Papillote 119
- Tangy Egg & Cheese Salad 120
- Mexican Bean Salad 121
- Easy Curried Coconut Lentils 122
- Vegan Lentil Chili 123
- Walnut Lentil Tacos 124
- Vegan Potato Curry 125
- Quinoa Enchiladas 126

APPETIZERS 128
- Sweet and Spicy Meatballs 128
- Brisket Sliders with Caramelized Onions 129
- Buffalo Chicken Dip 131
- Cilantro Lime Chicken Drumsticks 132
- Pizza Pull Apart Bread 133
- Cilantro Jalapeño Hummus 134

Artichoke & Spinach Dip Applebee's Copycat 135

Hawaiian Meatballs 136

Bacon Cheeseburger Dip 137

Sweet BBQ Meatballs 138

Easy Bacon Hot Dog Bites 139

DESSERTS 140

Chocolate Pots De Crème 140

Pumpkin Banana Chocolate Chip Bundt Cake 141

Apple Crisp 143

Molten Brownie Pudding 144

French Apple Cobbler 145

Bourbon Sticky Toffee Pudding 147

Apple Cinnamon Cake 149

Mini-Lemon Cheesecakes 151

INTRODUCTION

My passion for pressure cooking runs deep. If you have cooked with a pressure cooker, then you will be familiar with this kitchen appliance. It is a multi-cooker that performs more than functions. The Instant Pot enables you to cook a wide variety of dishes including meat, fish, eggs, grain, poultry, beans, cakes, yogurt and vegetables etc. What makes the Instant Pot exceptional is because you can use different cooking programs such as a steamer, rice cooker, sauté pan, and even a warming pot, thus saving more time, money, and space than buying any other kitchen appliances.

The Instant Pot serves as a multi-use programmable appliance can help create easy, fast and flavorful recipes with the ability to apply different cooking settings all in one pot. It was developed by clever Canadian technology experts seeking to be the ultimate kitchen mate, from stir-frying, pressure cooking, slow cooking and yogurt and cake making. It was created to serve as a one-stop shop to allow home cooks prepare a tasty meal with the press of a button. You can cook almost everything in your Instant Pot.

In this book, we will explore the variety of easy delicious dishes you can cook with your Instant Pot. We will explore a wide variety of dishes, from breakfast to dinner, soups to stews, desserts to appetizers, meat to beef, side dishes to vegetables and use a healthy ingredient in the process. The vast majority of the recipes can be prepared and served in less than 45 minutes. Each recipe is written with the exact preparation time, cooking instructions and ingredients required to prepare the dishes. Once you try these delicious dishes with our cookbook, you and your Instant Pot are sure to become inseparable too.

What is an Instant Pot?

The Instant Pot is a multifunctional cooker that acts as a slow cooker, rice cooker, steamer, electric pressure cooker, sauté pan and a yogurt maker. It is a single device or multi-cooker that does the job of seven different kitchen appliances ranging from electric pressure cooker, rice cooker, steamer, yogurt maker, sauté pan, and warming pot etc. It makes use of a combination of steam and pressure which enables your foods to cook quicker and safer than other devices. It is a programmable countertop multi-cooker which speeds up cooking by 2~6 times using up to 70% less energy.

The Instant Pot can cook nutritious healthy food in a convenient and consistent fashion, making everything from slow-and-low barbecue dishes and tenders stews to perfectly prepared rice pilaf, lentil, bacon, chicken and steamed veggies. You can rely on Instant Pot more than any other kitchen appliances and it deserves to earn a spot in your kitchen.

The Instant Pot is a versatile multi-cooker that can do the job of a pressure cooker, slow cooker, rice cooker, steamer, poultry and more. It has lots of safety features which makes it safer to use and comes in different models. It comes with preset programs that are specifically designed to cook your food to perfection, whether it be a cheesecake, a stew, soup, or porridge.

Benefits of Cooking with Your Instant Pot

1 Saving Time & Energy:

The Instant Pot cook foods much faster than any other traditional methods of cooking. Electric pressure cooker can reduce cooking time by up to 70% when compared with other methods. Cooking with an Instant Pot requires less water used in cooking and a fully insulated external pot, much less energy is required thereby saving up to 70% of energy comparing with boiling, steaming, and slow cooking.

You will save more time and money when cooking with an Instant Pot. A whole chicken can be cooked in just half an hour, make a tender pot roast in less than 2 hours, cook a large squash in just 10 minutes and veggies in less than 5 thereby saving more time and energy.

2 Preserving Nutrients & Cook Tasty Food:

Pressure cooking ensures that heat is evenly and quickly distributed. The food is not necessarily required to be immersed in water, it simply requires sufficient water to keep the pressure cooker filled with steam. This will not allow the vitamins and minerals to be leached or dissolved away by water. Since the food is surrounded by the steam, the foods will not be oxidized by air exposure at heat, so asparagus, lentil, broccoli, artichoke, and other veggies retain their bright green colors and phytochemical. It will also enable the food to retain its original flavor.

Scientific studies have proved that pressure cooking is the best method for retaining the vitamins and minerals of the food that your body needs. Pressure cooking broccoli, for instance, will retain 90% of its vitamin C. The retention when compared to boiling is (66% retention) or steaming (78%). Instant Pot tends to be the healthier option.

3 Eliminating Harmful Micro-Organisms in Food:

Pressure cookers cook foods at a temperature above the boiling point of water, killing almost all harmful living micro-organisms such as bacteria, fungi, and viruses. It helps to kill harmful micro-organisms that are toxic to our health. Some foods such as rice, wheat, corn and beans may carry fungal poisons called aflatoxins.

Aflatoxins are naturally occurring mycotoxins produced by many species of Aspergillus fungi, as a result of improper storage, such as in humid conditions. Research has proved that aflatoxins are a potent trigger of liver cancer and may play a vital role in a host of other cancers too. Aflatoxins cannot be destroyed by just heating your food to the boiling point, they can only be destroyed by pressure cooking.

4 Helps Boost Digestibility of Foods:

I believe you must have heard, "You are what you eat." But actually, you are what you absorb from your food. Boosting the digestibility of your food will maximize the nutritional value to your body. Pressure cooking makes even the toughest meats moist and tender, which is the key to foods that your body can easily digest.

Making Sense of Your Instant Pot Buttons

1 Soup:

The Instant Pot has a soup program that is 30 minutes on High Pressure. But this program depends on if you are using fresh or frozen meats. The soup times may range from 20 minutes to an hour. The soup function cooks at High Pressure for about 30 minutes. It can be Adjusted to more to cook for about 40 minutes. It can also be Adjusted to less to cook for about 20 minutes.

2 Meat / Stew:

The meat / stew program is 20 minutes on High Pressure. Though, the times may vary wildly depending on temperature, size, and thickness of the meats. The Meat / Stew function cooks at High Pressure for about 35 minutes. It can be Adjusted to more cooks for 45 minutes and Adjusted to less cooks for about 20 minutes.

3 Bean / Chili:

The Bean / Chili program is 30 minutes on High Pressure. The Bean / Chili button cooks at High Pressure for 30 minutes. It can be Adjusted to more cooks for about 40 minutes. The button can also be Adjusted to less cooks for about 25 minutes.

4 Poultry:

The poultry button is 12 minutes on High Pressure. This cooking time is meant for uncooked chicken in small portions. Larger chicken pieces will need a cooking time of about 25 minutes to reach a center temperature of 165°F. The Poultry function cooks at High Pressure for 15 minutes. The button can be Adjusted to more cooks for about 30 minutes and Adjusted to less cooks for about 5 minutes.

5 Slow Cook:

The Slow Cook button can be programmed from between 30 minutes to 20 hours. The pressure cooking time can be lowered up to 24 hours. The Slow Cook mode can be set to normal (which is equivalent to low), more (which is equivalent to high), or less (which is equivalent to keep warm mode).

6 Sauté:

The sauté button can be used to brown your meat directly inside of your Instant Pot. The temperature of the sauté button can be adjusted by using the 'Adjust' function to cycle through the modes of less, normal, and more. The temperature mode has to be adjusted within 10 seconds of pressing the sauté mode. When you press the Sauté function, kindly wait until it displays "Hot" before adding ingredients to the pot.

7 Pressure:

The pressure button serves as a toggle between low and High-Pressure modes. It can simply be used to switch between High and low-pressure settings for pressure cooking programs.

8 Manual:

The Manual button can be used to start pressure cooking. It can be switched between low and high pressure by using the 'pressure' button within 10 seconds of pressing the 'Manual' button. You can set a pressure level and cook time using the Adjust and [+] or [-] buttons. When the time is up, time will begin to count down.

9 Adjust:

This button can be used to adjust the temperature of the slow cooking and sauté settings between less, normal, and more. This button can be used to toggle from the Less, Normal and More settings on older Instant Pot versions. You can select any of the feature you wish to use and press Adjust until the light under Less, Normal and More is adjusted to the desired setting.

10 Timer:

The timer setting is for programmed delayed cooking. The button performs the function for both slow cooking mode and regular pressure cooking mode. This setting must be pressed within 10 seconds of setting your cooking program's time and can be adjusted by pressing the + and – buttons.

11 Keep warm / Cancel:

The Keep Warm button sets the unit into keep warm mode, and another less turns the unit OFF. This setting helps to turn the Auto Keep Warm function ON and OFF. The Keep Warm function keeps the foods in your cooking pot between 145–172°F. This button can also be used to cancel a function or to turn off the Instant Pot.

12 Yogurt:

This function is not included in the IP-LUX series and is a fully-automated program. These settings can be sued to make yogurt. You can press this button and Adjust to More for boiling the milk and use Normal for incubating the yogurt.

13 Steam:

This button cooks at High Pressure for about 10 minutes. It can be Adjusted to more cooks for about 15 minutes and Adjusted to less for about 3 minutes. The Steam function is simply normal High-Pressure mode that can be set all the way down to 0 minutes. It simply means that once the cooking time is up, you can perform a quick release. This function is very important when cooking leafy vegetables and preventing them from being overcooked.

14 Porridge and Multigrain:

The Porridge button cooks at High Pressure for 20 minutes. It can be Adjusted to more cooks for 30 minutes and Adjusted to less cooks for 15 minutes.

15 Multigrain:

The Multigrain button cooks at High Pressure for 40 minutes. It can be Adjusted to more cooks for 45 minutes and pressure cooking time of 60 minutes. It can also be Adjusted to less cooks for 20 minutes.

16 Rice:

The Rice button is an automated program that begins at 12 minutes. This button functions at low pressure and can cook white or jasmine rice in 20 minutes flat. The setting is specifically designed for cooking white rice and the cooking time can be adjusted depending on the quantity of water and rice in the cooking pot.

17 Egg:

The Egg button cooks at High Pressure for 5 minutes. The button can be Adjusted to more cooks for 6 minutes and Adjusted to less cooks for about 4 minutes.

18 Cake:

The Cake button cooks at High Pressure for 30 minutes. It can be Adjusted to more cooks for 40 minutes and Adjusted to less cooks for about 25 minutes.

Instant Pot Accessories (Must-Have Tools)

The Instant Pot comes along with lots of accessories. You might need to buy more accessories to get the most out of your meals:

1. **Silicone Egg Mold:**

The silicon egg mold will work in your 5, 6, 8-quart pressure cookers. It can be used for storing smaller portions and includes a sealing lid.

2. **Silicone Mini Mitts:**

It is advisable to protect your fingers with the mini mitts. The cooking pot usually gets hot when cooking, the mini mitts set can be used to protect your hands when lifting items out of your pressure cooker.

3. **Silicone Vegetable Steamer and Lifter:**

The steamer / lifter keeps your veggies off the heated bottom of your pressure cooker. The steamer handles can be used to lift items easily from the pressure cooker. It also works great in your microwave. It can be used to lift a whole chicken out of your Instant Pot without it falling apart.

4. **7-inch Spring Form Non-Stick Pan:**

The spring form pan can be used for baking. It is great for baking cakes, cheesecakes, and bread. These sizes will fit into your pressure cooker 5, 6, 8 quarts.

5. **Cook's Stainless-Steel Steamer Basket / Colander:**

Most pressure cookers don't come with this basket! These tool helps to keep your food items off the bottom heating element and out of the water. Food items such as pasta do not require draining when cooking in a pressure cooker but having the pasta in this basket helps to easily lift the pasta from the pressure cooker.

6. **Clear lid:**

The clear lid comes with a steam vent and handle. It is used for sautéing or slow-cooking. It comes in 3, 6, and 8-quart sizes.

7. **Extra Silicone Rings:**

The extra silicone rings are needed on hand at all times. It can be used to switch out rings depending on whether you're cooking a sweet or savory dish. They usually wear out after multiple uses, but it's helpful an extra just in case.

8. **Steaming Rack:**

The steaming rack can be used to steam your veggies, pot-stickers, proteins, anything!

9. **Mesh steaming basket:**

This is another helpful variation of a steamer. The mesh steaming basket can be used for steaming, frying, straining. It can be used for many things and functions out of just one product.

10. **Extra Stainless Steel:**

It makes it easier to prepare multiple dishes. You just have to switch out the pots rather than cleaning one over and over again.

11. **Cheesecake pan:**

The cheesecake pan can be used for making cheesecake in your Instant Pot. Yep, it's true. Plus, the bottom is removable but doesn't leak can be used for dessert after steaming all the veggies.

12. **Instant Read Digital Meat Thermometer:**

This thermometer can used for measuring the heat content in meat. Having the Meat Thermometer on hand puts an end to serving undercooked or over cooked protein. It can also be used for daily cooking or grilling.

How to Clean Your Instant Pot (Cleaning Tips)

It is important to clean your Instant Pot right after dinner or right after you're done using it, because:

- The spills, drips, etc. are still warm and clean up more easily when cleaning right away.
- You'll appreciate it being clean the next time you're ready to use it.

What NOT to do when cleaning your Instant Pot:

Ensure that you clean your Instant Pot right after cook and avoid the following practices when cleaning:

- Do not submerge the base in water.
- Do not leave it plugged in while cleaning it.

Tools you will need when cleaning your Instant Pot include:

- Washcloth
- Non-scratch scouring pad
- Towel
- Dish soap or all-purpose spray cleaner
- Vinegar
- Baking soda
- Toothbrush or small cleaning brushes

How to Clean Your Instant Pot:

1. Fill a sink with hot, soapy water. This step is the most important because it will make everything easier and faster.

2. Ensure that you unplug your Instant Pot and remove the insert pot from the base.

3. The next step is to place everything that needs to be cleaned in the hot, soapy water. Dump out any liquid that must have accumulated in the condensation cup. Place the silicone ring, valve cover if your model has a removable valve cover, sealing valve, and lid in the soapy water.

4. Dip a small cleaning utensil such as toothbrush or small cleaning brush in the hot, soapy water. Use the brush to clean all the nooks and crannies of the base. Make use of a wet, wrung-out cloth in sopping up any liquids or dislodged food particles. The toothbrush and the washcloth can be uses to reach and dislodge everything.

5. Use a washcloth and all-purpose spray cleaner to wipe down the outside of the Instant Pot to look pretty and shiny.

6. Wash everything that's been soaking in the hot, soapy water. After washing, rinse and air dry with the towel.

7. Scrub the silicone ring with the toothbrush. Use baking soda to remove any odor and staining. You can soak the silicon ring in vinegar water for a few hours if it's still stinky. Rinse and air dry after washing.

8. Scrub the inside of the insert pot in circular motion with non-scratch scouring pad. Make use of baking soda for stubborn messes.

9. Scrub the following accessories with toothbrush — the lid, sealing valve, condensation cup and wipe with a towel.

Instant Pot FAQ – Frequently Asked Questions

Before Purchasing Instant Pot

The answers to Frequently Asked Questions before purchasing an Instant Pot are listed below:

1. What is an Instant Pot? Is it the same as a pressure cooker?

Yes, the Instant Pot is the same as the pressure cooker and is currently one of the most popular electric pressure cooker brands. It is a multi-functional cooker and has some extra functions such as rice cooker, soup, poultry, meat, yogurt, sauté pan etc.

2. Does the Instant Pot really speed up the cooking process?

Pressure cooking is always faster and saves time. The fast cooking process may not be noticeable for some foods like broccoli or shrimps. Foods such as pulled pork can be done in under 90 minutes, when it usually takes about 2 to 4 hours to make in the oven.

3. Are there any disadvantages with cooking in the Instant Pot?

The disadvantage involved in cooking with any pressure cooker is you can't inspect, taste, or adjust the food along the way. That's why it's necessary to follow the exact recipes instructions with accurate cooking times.

4. Is Instant Pot safe to use?

Most modern electric pressure cookers like the Instant Pot are quiet, very safe and easy to use. The Instant Pot has about 10 UL Certified proven safety mechanisms to avoid some of the potential issues. It has lots of safety features to prevent potential issues.

5. What is Instant Pot's working pressure?

The Instant Pot working pressure is within the range of 10.15~11.6 psi.

6. Can Instant Pot be used for Pressure Canning?

No, the Instant Pot has not been tested for food safety in pressure canning. The cooking programs in Instant Pot IP-CSG, IP-LUX and IP-DUO series are regulated by a pressure sensor instead of a thermometer, the elevation of your location can disrupt the actual cooking temperature. For that very reason, it is not advisable to use your Instant Pot for pressure canning purpose.

7. Can I use the Instant Pot for Pressure Frying?

We would not recommend pressure frying in any electric pressure cookers. The pressure cooker gasket may be melted by the splattering oil.

After Purchasing Instant Pot

1. What kind of Instant Pot accessories do you recommend?

There is hand-picked list of accessories we would recommend. The accessories include steamer baskets, meat thermometers, silicon egg mold, cheesecake pan, steaming rack etc.

2. What kind of accessories or containers can I use in the Instant Pot?

Any oven-safe accessories and containers can be used in your Instant Pot. Always have in mind that different materials will conduct heat differently and this will make the cooking times to vary. Always use stainless steel containers as they quickly conduct heat.

3. I just got my Instant Pot. What should I do first?

Congratulations and welcome to the party! Conduct an initial test run before cooking with your Instant Pot.

4. How to do a Quick Release?

When the cooking cycle is up, carefully move the venting knob from sealing position to venting position. It usually takes a few minutes and rapidly releases the pressure in the pressure cooker. Exercise some patient and wait until the floating valve completely drops before opening the lid.

5. How to do a Natural Release?

When the cooking cycle is up, you have to wait until the floating valve completely drops before opening the lid. Carefully turn the venting knob from sealing position to venting position. It will enable all the pressure to release before opening the lid. Natural pressure release usually takes about 10 – 25 minutes.

Troubleshooting Tips

Here is a list of instructions to carry out when troubleshooting:

1. **Rice is half cooked or too hard:**

Possible Reason: The rice contained too little water

Solution: Ensure that the dry rice and water ratio is adjusted according to recipe instructions.

Possible Reason: The Instant Pot lid is removed too early

Solution: When the cooking cycle is up, leave the lid on for additional 5 minutes.

2. **Rice is too soft:**

Possible Reason: The rice contained too much water.

Solution: Ensure that the dry rice and water ratio is adjusted according to recipe instructions.

3. **Difficulty with closing lid:**

Possible Reason: The sealing ring is not properly closed.

Solution: Carefully position the sealing ring to stay tightly in place.

Possible Reason: The float valve may be in popped-up position.

Solution: Gently press down the float to stay in place.

4. **Difficulty with opening lid:**

Possible Reason: Pressure inside the cooker

Solution: When the cooking cycle is complete, position the steam release handle to the venting position to release the internal pressure. Carefully remove the lid after the pressure is completely released.

Possible Reason: The float valve stuck at the popped-up position thereby causing difficulties in opening the lid.

Solution: Carefully press the float valve with a pen or long utensil to open the lid.

5. **Float valve unable to rise:**

Possible Reason: This may result when there is too little food or water in inner pot.

Solution: Pour water according to the recipe instructions.

Possible Reason: The float valve may be blocked by the lid locking pin.

Solution: Completed close the lid completely to prevent the steam from coming out from the steam valve.

Possible Reason: The Steam release valve may not be placed in sealing position.

Solution: Move the steam release handle to the sealing position.

6. **Steam leaks from the side of the lid:**

Possible Reason: There is no sealing ring in place.

Solution: Carefully install the sealing ring in place.

Possible Reason: The sealing ring might also be damaged.

Solution: Replace the damaged sealing ring with a new one.

Possible Reason: There might be some particles of food debris attached to the sealing ring.

Solution: Clean the sealing ring to remove any attached food debris.

7. **Steam leaks from float valve for over 2 minutes:**

Possible Reason: Some particles of food debris may be attached on the float valve silicone seal.

Solution: Clean the float valve silicone seal to remove any attached food debris.

Possible Reason: The float valve silicone ring may be worn- out.

Solution: Replace the worn-out float valve silicone ring with a new one.

BREAKFAST

Bacon and Egg Risotto

Servings: 2

Preparation time: 5 minutes

Cook time: 5 minutes

Total time: 10 minutes

Ingredients:

- 3 slices of center cut bacon, chopped
- 1/3 cup of chopped onion
- ¾ cup of Arborio rice
- 3 tbsp. of dry white wine
- 1 ½ cups of chicken broth
- 2 eggs
- 2 tbsp. of grated parmesan cheese
- Salt and pepper, to taste
- Chives, for garnish

Cooking Instructions:

1. Set your Instant Pot to "Sauté" and add the bacon.

2. Cook the bacon until fat begins to render and bacon is crisping for about 5 minutes. Stir in the onion and sauté for about 2 to 3 minutes. Stir in the rice and sauté for additional 1 minute.

3. Pour in the wine and give everything a good stir. Deglaze the pot by scraping up any browned bits from the bottom of the pot.

4. Add the chicken broth when the wine has been absorbed and stir. Secure the lid in place and ensure that the valve is in sealing position.

5. Select Manual function to cook on High Pressure for 5 minutes. When the timer beeps, do a natural pressure release.

6. Carefully remove the lid and stir in the Parmesan. Add salt and pepper to taste. Divide between two bowls, add the cooked egg, and sprinkle with chives.

7. Serve and enjoy!

Strawberry Trail Mix Oatmeal

Preparation time: 5 minutes

Cook time: 10 minutes

Total time: 15 minutes

Servings: 2

Ingredients:

- 1 cup of steel cut oats
- 1.5 cups of water
- 2 tablespoons of butter
- 1 cup of freshly squeezed orange juice
- 1 tablespoon of dried cranberries
- 1 tablespoon of raisins
- 1 tablespoon of chopped dried apricots
- 2 tablespoons of pure maple syrup
- ¼ teaspoon of ground cinnamon
- 2 tablespoons of chopped pecans
- 1/8 teaspoon of salt
- Tasty toppings: ½ - 1 cup of chopped strawberries, extra cinnamon, extra pecans, milk or almond milk and granola

Cooking Instructions:

1. Spritz your Instant Pot inner liner with spray oil.

2. Melt the butter and add that to the bottom of the pot. Add all ingredients (except for toppings) into the bottom of your Instant Pot and stir to combine.

3. Secure the lid in place. Select the Manual function to cook on High Pressure for 10 minutes. When the time is up, do a quick pressure release.

4. Carefully remove the lid and stir oatmeal. Spoon the cooked oats into two serving plates and add your desired toppings.

5. Serve and enjoy!

Breakfast Hash

Serves: 4

Preparation time: 10 minutes

Cook time: 1 minute

Total time: 11 minutes

Ingredients:

- Cooking oil
- 6 small potatoes, peeled
- 6 eggs
- ¼ cup of water
- 1 cup of shredded American cheese
- 1 cup of chopped breakfast ham

Cooking Instructions:

1. Press the "Sauté" function on your Instant Pot and add a layer of oil.

2. Shred your potatoes in a food processor and squeeze out any excess moisture. Add the shredded potatoes to the hot oil.

3. Allow the potatoes to brown in the hot oil without stirring. In a medium bowl, beat the eggs and reserve.

4. Break up the potatoes with a wooden spoon when browned. Add the water, eggs, cheese, and ham. Give everything a good stir.

5. Secure the lid in place. Select Manual High Pressure for 1 minute. Do a quick pressure release and carefully open the lid.

6. Serve immediately with toast, if desired.

Spanish Chorizo & Potato Hash

Preparation time: 5 minutes

Cook time: 15 minutes

Total time: 20 minutes

Servings: 4

Ingredients:

- 6 large potatoes
- 1 chorizo sausage
- 4 slices back bacon
- 1 large onion, peeled and diced
- 250 g soft cheese
- 2 tablespoons of Greek yoghurt
- 1 tablespoon of puree
- 1 tablespoon of olive oil
- 200 ml vegetable stock
- 3 tablespoons of rosemary
- 3 tablespoons of basil
- Salt & pepper

Cooking Instructions:

1. Add the onion, garlic and olive oil into the bottom of your Instant Pot.

2. Set your Instant Pot on Sauté function and cook until the onions become soft. Peel and dice the potatoes.

3. Thinly slice the sausages and add to the pot. Slice the bacon into chunks and add to the pot. Add the seasoning and sauté for some minutes.

4. Add the stock and secure the lid in place. Select the Soup setting for 10 minutes. When the timer beeps, do a natural pressure release.

5. Carefully remove the lid. In a medium bowl, add a little bit more herbs and mix in the soft cheese and Greek yoghurt.

6. Add the mixture to your pot and give everything a good stir.

7. Serve and enjoy!

Apple Bread with Salted Caramel Icing

Cook time: 1 hour 10 minutes

Total time: 1 hour 10 minutes

Servings: 10

Calories: 551 kcal

Ingredients:

- 3 cups apples, peeled, cored, and cubed
- 1 cup of sugar
- 2 eggs
- 1 tablespoon of vanilla
- 1 tablespoon of apple pie spice
- 2 cups of flour
- 1 stick butter
- 1 tablespoon of baking powder

For the Topping:

- 1 stick salted butter
- 2 cups of brown sugar
- 1 cup of heavy cream
- 2 cups of powdered sugar

Cooking Instructions:

1. Cream together eggs, butter, apple pie spice, and sugar until creamy and smooth in your mixer.

2. Stir in the 3 cups of apples. In a medium bowl, mix together the flour and baking powder. Add the flour mix to your wet mix.

3. Add the thick batter mixture into your 7" spring form pan. Add the trivet into the bottom of your Instant pot and pour 1 cup of water.

4. Add the pan on the trivet and secure the lid in place. Select Manual High Pressure for 70 minutes.

5. Do a quick release. Carefully open the lid and top with Icing.

6. Serve and enjoy!

French Toast Casserole

Preparation time: 10 minutes

Cook time: 15 minutes

Total time: 25 minutes

Ingredients:

- 3 eggs
- 1 cup of half and half cream
- ½ cup of milk
- 1 tbsp. of cinnamon
- 1 tsp. of vanilla
- 1 loaf of French bread cubed
- ½ cup of blueberries, or more to taste

Cooking Instructions:

1. Spray your Instant Pot inner liner with cooking spray.

2. Cube bread and add into your Instant Pot.

3. In a medium bowl, whisk together milk, cream, cinnamon, vanilla and eggs. Pour the custard mixture over the bread cubes.

4. Turn the bread to coat completely with the mixture. Sprinkle in the blueberries before lock the lid in place.

5. Select Manual High Pressure for 15 minutes. Do a natural pressure release for about 15 minutes. Carefully remove the lid.

6. Serve and enjoy!

Breakfast Cobbler

Serves: 2

Preparation time: 10 minutes

Cook time: 10 minutes

Total time: 20 minutes

Ingredients:

- 1 pear, diced
- 1 apple, diced
- 1 plum, diced
- 2 tablespoon (30 ml) local honey
- 3 tablespoons (45 ml) coconut oil
- ½ tsp. of ground cinnamon
- ¼ cup (19 g) unsweetened shredded coconut
- ¼ cup (30 g) pecan pieces
- 2 tablespoons of (20 g) sunflower seeds (salted and roasted)
- Optional garnish: coconut whipped cream

Cooking Instructions:

1. Add the cut fruit into the Instant Pot inner liner.

2. Add honey and coconut oil, sprinkle the cinnamon. Secure the lid in place and ensure that the valve is in sealing position.

3. Select the Steam function to cook for about 10 minutes. When the timer beeps, use a quick pressure release.

4. Carefully open the lid and transfer the cooked fruit with a slotted spoon into a serving bowl. Add the coconut, pecans, and sunflower seeds into the residual liquid.

5. Set your Instant Pot on Sauté function. Let the contents to cook, shifting them regularly to prevent burning.

6. When they are browned for about 5 minutes, remove them and top your cooked fruit.

7. Serve warm and topped with coconut whipped cream if desired.

Ham & Egg Casserole

Preparation time: 10 minutes

Cook time: 15 minutes

Total time: 25 minutes

Ingredients:

- 4 medium red potatoes
- ½ onion, diced
- 1 cup of chopped ham
- 2 cups of shredded cheddar cheese
- 10 large eggs
- 1 cup milk
- 1 tsp. of salt
- 1 tsp. of pepper

Cooking Instructions:

1. Spray your Instant Pot insert with nonstick cooking spray.

2. Add the eggs and milk into the insert. Give everything a good whisk until well blended.

3. Add the potatoes, ham, onions, cheese, and salt and pepper in with the eggs.

4. Give everything a good mix to cover with the egg mixture. Cover the bowl with a piece of foil.

5. Add the steam rack into the bottom of your Instant Pot and pour 2 cups of water. Place the bowl covered with foil on top of the steam rack.

6. Secure the lid in place. Select Manual function to cook on High Pressure for 25 minutes.

7. When the time is up, do a quick pressure release. Carefully open the lid.

8. Serve with your desired toppings like sour cream, salsa, avocado, more cheese tomatoes, and salt and pepper!

Quinoa Blueberry Breakfast Bowl

Preparation time: 5 minutes

Cook time: 1 minute

Total time: 6 minutes

Servings: 4

Calories: 400 kcal

Ingredients:

- 1 ½ cups of white quinoa
- 1 ½ cups of water
- 1 cinnamon stick
- ¼ cup of raisins
- 1 tbsp. of honey, plus more for serving
- ¾ cup of grated apple
- 1 cup of cold-pressed apple juice
- 1 cup of plain yogurt, plus more for serving
- ¼ cup of chopped pistachios
- Blueberries to serve

Cooking Instructions:

1. First, rinse the quinoa in a fine mesh strainer.

2. Add the quinoa, water and cinnamon stick into the bottom of your Instant Pot.

3. Secure the lid in place and ensure that the valve is in sealing position.

4. When the timer beeps, use a natural pressure release for about 10 minutes, then quick release any remaining pressure.

5. Carefully open the lid and spoon the quinoa out into bowl. Slowly remove the cinnamon stick and let to cool.

6. Add the raisins, honey, apple and apple juice and give everything a good stir to combine.

7. Refrigerate for at least 1 hour or overnight. Add the yogurt and stir to combine.

8. Serve topped with yogurt, pistachios, blueberries and honey!

Western Omelets Quiche

Serve: 4

Preparation time: 10 minutes

Cook time: 30 minutes

Total time: 40 minutes

Ingredients:

- 6 large eggs, well beaten
- ½ cup half and half
- 1/8 tsp. of THM Himalayan High Mineral Salt
- 1/8 tsp. of ground black pepper
- 6-8 oz. Canadian Bacon, chopped
- ½ - ¾ cup of diced peppers, red, green and orange
- 3-4 organic spring onions, thinly sliced, reserving tops for garnish
- ¾ cup of shredded cheese
- 1/8 – ¼ cup of shredded cheese to garnish (optional)

Cooking Instructions:

1. Add the trivet into the bottom of your Instant Pot and pour 1 ½ cups of water.

2. Spray your soufflé dish, set aside. In a medium bowl, whisk together the eggs, milk, salt and pepper.

3. Add the diced Canadian bacon, diced colored peppers, spring onion slices, and cheese to the soufflé dish and give everything a good mix.

4. Pour the egg mixture over the meat and give everything a good stir to combine. Loosely cover the soufflé dish with aluminum foil.

5. Place the dish in the Instant Pot liner. Secure the lid in place and ensure that the valve is in sealing position.

6. Select Manual High Pressure for 30 minutes. When the pot timer beeps, do a quick pressure release. Carefully remove the lid and remove the soufflé dish.

7. Open the foil and sprinkle the top of the western quiche with additional cheese. Garnish with chopped spring onion tops.

8. Serve and enjoy!

Cinnamon Brown Rice Pudding

Preparation time: 5 minutes

Cook time: 35 minutes

Total time: 40 minutes

Servings: 4

Ingredients:

- 1 cup of short grain brown rice
- 1 ½ cups of water
- 1 tbsp. of vanilla extract
- 1 cinnamon stick
- 1 tablespoon of butter
- 1 cup of raisins
- 3 tablespoons of honey
- ½ cup of heavy cream

Cooking Instructions:

1. Add the rice, water, vanilla, cinnamon stick, and butter into the bottom of your Instant Pot.

2. Secure the lid in place and ensure that the valve is in sealing position.

3. Select Manual High Pressure for 20 minutes. When the timer beeps, do a quick pressure release.

4. Carefully open the lid and remove the cinnamon stick.

5. Discard the cinnamon stick and stir in raisins, honey and cream.

6. Set your Instant Pot to Sauté function adjust to less. Simmer for about for 5 minutes.

7. Serve warm and enjoy!

Breakfast Burrito Casserole

Preparation time: 10 minutes

Cook time: 13 minutes

Total time: 23 minutes

Serves: 6 tacos

Ingredients:

- 4 eggs
- 2 lb. red potatoes, cubed
- ¼ cup of chopped white or yellow onion
- 1 diced jalapeno
- 6 ounces ham steak, cubed
- ½ teaspoon of salt
- ½ teaspoon of mesquite seasoning
- ¼ teaspoon of chili powder
- ¾ teaspoon of taco seasoning
- Burrito toppings like: Salsa, avocado, hot sauce and marinated red onions.
- Tortillas

Cooking Instructions:

1. In a large bowl, mix together the salt, seasonings and eggs and 1 tbsp. of water.

2. Gently beat the egg until the yokes are broken up. Add the onions, potatoes or cheese, ham and jalapeno to a bowl and cover the bowl with a foil.

3. Pour 1 cup of water into the bottom of your Instant Pot. Add the covered bowl with the foil into your trivet.

4. Place the trivet into your Instant Pot. Secure the lid in place and ensure that the valve is in sealing position.

5. Select Manual High Pressure for 13 minutes. When the timer beeps, do a natural pressure release. Carefully open the lid and remove the bowl.

6. Fill your burritos! Heat the tortillas in a skillet for a few seconds on each side. Add a few scoops of the egg mixtures, a slice pf avocado, salsa and red onions in each burrito.

7. Serve and enjoy!

SOUPS & STEWS
Red Pepper Tomato Soup

Preparation time: 10 minutes

Cook time: 5 minutes

Total time: 15 minutes

Ingredients:

- 1 tbsp. of butter
- 1 tbsp. of oil
- 2 white onions, diced
- 8 red bell peppers, diced
- 8 cloves garlic
- 4 medium tomatoes (or 2 canned fire roasted tomatoes)
- 2 tsp. of herbes de provence
- ½ tsp. of paprika
- ¼ tsp. of cayenne pepper
- 2-3 cups of bone or vegetable broth
- ½ tsp. of salt
- ½ tsp. of pepper
- Parsley or Cilantro for garnish

Cooking Instructions:

1. Set your Instant Pot on Sauté function and add the butter and oil.

2. Sauté onions for a couple of minutes until they soften. Mince the garlic gloves (or use jarred), add to pressure cooker.

3. Add the red peppers, diced tomatoes (or use canned) into the pot. Add herbes de Provence, paprika, cayenne pepper, salt, and pepper.

4. Give everything a good stir to combine and let cook about 2 to 3 minutes. Add 2 cups of broth and give everything a good stir.

5. Secure the lid in place and ensure that the valve is in sealing position. Select Manual High Pressure for 5 minutes. When the timer beeps, do a quick pressure release.

6. Blend soup with immersion blender or remove to process in a blender. Add rest of the broth as required to achieve your desired consistency.

7. Season with more salt and pepper to taste. Serve with your desired toppings like chopped fresh toppings such as cucumbers, onions, squash, zucchini, cheese and sour cream.

8. Serve immediately and enjoy!

Spanish Infused Chicken Stew

Preparation time: 10 minutes

Cook time: 3 hours

Total time: 3 hours 10 minutes

Ingredients:

- 4 large chicken breasts, cut into chunks
- 4 cloves of garlic, minced
- ½ cooking chorizo, chopped
- 2 carrots, chopped
- 2 courgettes, chopped
- 2 leeks, chopped
- 3 red skinned potatoes, scrubbed and chopped in half
- 1 can of cannellini beans
- 1 handful of parsley, chopped
- A small handful of oregano, finely chopped
- Glass of fino sherry or dry white wine, and one for yourself
- A large pinch of smoked paprika
- A couple of strands of saffron
- Salt and pepper to taste
- Chicken stock, plenty to cover the chicken and vegetables

Cooking Instructions:

1. Prepare your vegetables and add them into the bottom of your Instant Pot.

2. Heat some oil in a sauté pan and cook the garlic, chicken and chorizo until the chicken is browned.

3. Add the chicken, chorizo and garlic mixture into your Instant Pot and give everything a good stir.

4. Lightly heat the stock and add the herbs, spices and seasonings. Pour over the chicken to cover.

5. Secure the lid in place and ensure that the valve is in sealing position. Slow cook for 3 hours.

6. When the timer beeps, do a natural pressure release. Carefully open the lid and adjust the seasoning to taste.

7. Serve with crusty bread or rice and enjoy!

Italian Wedding Soup

Preparation time: 10 minutes

Cook time: 10 minutes

Total time: 20 minutes

Ingredients:

- 1 3-4 lb. whole chicken
- 1 cup of large cut up carrots
- 1 head of escarole
- 1 28 ounces can of diced tomatoes
- 32 ounces chicken broth
- 10 meat ball cut in quarters
- 2 celery stalks, chopped
- ½ lb. your desired pasta

Cooking Instructions:

1. Add the whole chicken into the bottom of your Instant Pot and pour 2 cups of water.

2. Secure the lid in place and ensure that the valve is in sealing position. Select Poultry function to cook for about 20 minutes.

3. When the timer beeps, do a natural pressure release. Carefully open the lid and remove the chicken. Remove the bones off the chicken.

4. Add the meat in your Instant Pot. Add the carrots, celery, full can of tomatoes, and chicken broth and your meatballs quartered. Secure the lid in place.

5. Select the Soup function to cook for 10 minutes. When the timer beeps, do a natural pressure release.

6. Carefully open the lid and set your Instant Pot on Sauté setting. Add in your pasta and Escarole. Secure the lid and select the Soup function for 2 more minutes.

7. When the timer beeps, do a quick pressure release. Carefully open the lid and give everything a good stir.

8. Serve and enjoy!

Andouille Sausage Stew

Serving: 6

Preparation time: 10 minutes

Cook time: 20 minutes

Total time: 30 minutes

Ingredients:

- 1 lb. of uncooked Pork Andouille Sausage, crumbled
- 1 medium sweet onion, halved and thinly sliced
- ½ lb. of grape or cherry tomatoes
- 1 ½ lb. of Yukon Gold potatoes, peeled and cut into 1" pieces
- ¾ lb. of collard greens, stems removed and thinly sliced
- 1 cup of chicken broth
- 1 tsp. of kosher salt
- 20 - 25 turns freshly ground black pepper
- ½ medium lemon, freshly squeezed

Cooking Instructions:

1. Set your Instant Pot to Sauté setting.

2. Add the crumbled Andouille sausage and cook for about 6 minutes, stirring occasionally. Add the sliced onions and tomatoes.

3. Give everything a good mix and continue to cook for another 3 to 4 minutes. Add the potatoes, collard greens and broth along with salt and pepper.

4. Secure the lid in place and ensure that the valve is in sealing position. Select Manual, High Pressure for 10 minutes.

5. Carefully open the lid and add fresh lemon juice. Adjust the seasoning with salt and pepper to taste.

6. Serve and enjoy!

Hearty Broccoli Soup

Prep time: 30 minutes

Cook time: 6 minutes

Total time: 36 minutes

Serves: 8-10

Ingredients:

- 1 tablespoon of vegan margarine or vegetable oil
- 1 small white onion, diced
- 3 cloves garlic, diced
- 64 ounces mushroom broth (like Pacific Foods Organic Mushroom broth - 2 boxes)
- 1 cup of water
- 1 cup of Unsweetened Almond milk, or other unsweetened non-dairy milk
- 2 large bunches of broccoli (4 heads), florets only
- 1 head of cauliflower, florets only
- 1 medium sized Japanese Yam or Yukon gold potato, peeled and cut into chunks
- 2 cups of prepared brown rice
- 1 pkg. Beyond Meat Lightly Seasoned Chicken Strips, thawed and diced
- 1 chicken flavored bouillon cube (we used Not-Chick'n by Edward and Sons)
- 2 tablespoons of low sodium Tamari (or gluten free lite soy sauce)
- ½ teaspoon of salt
- 3 teaspoons of nutritional yeast (opt.)
- 1 teaspoon of Spike seasoning
- A dash of black pepper

Cooking Instructions:

1. Press the Sauté function and add the margarine to melt.

2. When the margarine melts, add the diced onion. Cook the contents until softened, stirring occasionally.

3. Add garlic and cook for additional 1 minute. Press Cancel on Pot to turn off. Add the broccoli, yam/potato and cauliflower florets.

4. Add the tamari, salt, pepper, spike, nutritional yeast, and bouillon cube. Add the broth, milk, and water into the bottom of your Instant Pot.

5. Secure the lid in place and ensure that the valve is in sealing position. Select Manual High Pressure for 6 minutes.

6. When the timer beeps, do a natural pressure release. Carefully open the lid and use an immersion blender to puree the soup.

7. Stir in your cooked brown rice and vegan chicken when your desired consistency is achieved.

8. Serve and enjoy!

Italian Beef Stew

Preparation time: 10 minutes

Cook time: 35 minutes

Total time: 45 minutes

Yield: 6-8

Ingredients:

- 3 pounds of beef stew meat OR 2 pounds of ground beef, browned.
- 1 onion, diced
- 4 carrots, sliced
- 8 ounces fresh baby portabella mushrooms (optional)
- 24 ounces beef broth
- 15 ounces can diced tomatoes
- 3 tablespoons of flour
- 1 teaspoon of dried basil leaves
- 1 teaspoon of dried thyme leaves
- 1 teaspoon of salt
- 1 teaspoon of pepper Dried parsley

Cooking Instructions:

1. Add the meat into the bottom of your Instant Pot. If using ground beef, sauté then drain grease.

2. Add the carrots, broth, flour, basil, thyme, salt, pepper and diced tomatoes and give everything a good stir.

3. Secure the lid in place and ensure that the valve is in sealing position.

4. Select Manual, High Pressure for 35 minutes. When the timer beeps, do a quick pressure release.

5. Carefully open the lid and stir in mushrooms.

6. Serve and enjoy!

White Bean Parmesan Soup

Serves: 10

Preparation time: 10 minutes

Cook time: 5 minutes

Total time: 15 minutes

Ingredients:

- 1 tablespoon of olive oil
- 1 yellow onion, diced
- 6 cloves of minced garlic
- 6 cups of vegetable broth
- 1 can diced tomatoes, drained
- 1 tsp. of sugar
- ¾ cup of fresh grated parmesan cheese
- 1 tablespoon of Italian seasoning
- 1 teaspoon of salt
- ½ teaspoon of black pepper
- 4 cans of cannellini beans, drained and rinsed
- 6 ounces chopped spinach

Cooking Instructions:

1. Set your Instant Pot to Sauté function and add olive oil.

2. Add the onion and garlic. Stir until onion is translucent.

3. Add broth, tomatoes, sugar, cheese, Italian seasoning, salt, pepper, beans and spinach.

4. Secure the lid in place and ensure that the valve is in sealing position. Select Manual High Pressure for 5 minutes.

5. When the timer beeps, do a natural pressure release.

6. Carefully remove the lid and give everything a good stir.

7. Serve and enjoy!

Spicy Ethiopian Stew

Preparation time: 10 minutes

Cook time: 15 minutes

Total time: 25 minutes

Servings: 6

Ingredients:

- 1½ cups of dried lentils
- 3 large garlic cloves, minced
- 3 tbsp. of tomato paste
- 3-5 tsp. of Berbera Spice
- 5 cups of vegetable broth
- 1 yellow onion, chopped
- 2 ½ cups of butternut squash, cut into chunks
- ½ tsp. of sea salt
- ½ tbsp. of maple syrup
- 2 tbsp. of pureed ginger
- 1/2 (10 oz.) bag chopped frozen spinach

Cooking Instructions:

1. Dump all the ingredients into the bottom of your Instant Pot.

2. Secure the lid in place and ensure that the valve is in sealing position.

3. Select Manual, High Pressure for 15 minutes.

4. When the timer beeps, do a natural pressure release.

5. Serve and enjoy!

Creamy Thai Coconut Chicken Soup

Preparation time: 5 minutes

Cook time: 6 minutes

Total time: 11 minutes

Servings: 4

Calories: 443 kcal

Ingredients:

- 2 tbsp. of oil
- 1 small onion, quartered
- 2 pounds of skinless and boneless chicken breast or chicken thighs cut into cubes
- 2 tbsp. of Thai red curry paste Mae Ploy brand
- 1 red bell pepper, cut into thick strips
- 6 slices galangal, optional
- 6 kaffir lime leaves torn and bruised, optional
- 3 cups of chicken broth
- 2 tbsp. of fish sauce or salt to taste
- 1 heaping tbsp. of sugar
- ¾ cup of coconut milk
- 2 ½ tbsp. of lime juice
- Cilantro leaves

Cooking Instructions:

1. Set your Instant Pot to Sauté setting and add the oil.

2. Add the onion and cook for about 10 seconds. Add the chicken and sauté until the surface turns white.

3. Add the Thai curry paste, bell peppers, galangal and kaffir lime leaves (if desired). Give everything a good mix.

4. Add the chicken broth, fish sauce and sugar. Secure the lid in place and ensure that the valve is in sealing position.

5. Select Manual High Pressure for 6 minutes. When the timer beeps, do a quick pressure release. Carefully open the lid and add the coconut milk and lime juice.

6. Give everything a good stir to combine. Serve with cilantro and enjoy!

Tomato Chick Pea Soup

Preparation time: 10 minutes

Cook time: 3 minutes

Total time: 13 minutes

Ingredients:

- 3 tbsp. of olive oil
- 2 onions, diced
- 3 celery stalks, diced
- 3 carrots, diced
- 1 red bell pepper, diced
- 1 tbsp. of turmeric
- 1 tbsp. of ground coriander
- 1 tsp. of ground cinnamon
- 1 garlic clove (minced)
- 28-30 oz. of canned or fresh tomatoes
- 1 zucchini
- 2-3 cups of broth (vegetable or bone)
- 2 cans of chickpeas (garbanzo beans)
- Salt and pepper
- Garnish with Lime wedges, green onions or cilantro (optional)

Cooking Instructions:

1. Press the Sauté function on your Instant Pot and add butter and oil.

2. Add the onions and carrots and cook for about 4 to 6 minutes until the onions become translucent.

3. Add the celery and red bell pepper, along with the dry spices. Stir in the garlic, tomatoes, and zucchini. Rinse the chickpeas and add to mixture.

4. Add enough broth to cover vegetables and set some aside. Add salt and pepper to taste. Secure the lid in place and ensure that the valve is in sealing position.

5. Select Manual High Pressure for 3 minutes. When the timer beeps, do a quick pressure release. Carefully open the lid and add additional broth if desired. Give everything a good stir.

6. Squeeze the lime over the top or offer lime wedges with soup plates and serve immediately.

Beef & Butternut Squash Stew

Preparation time: 15 minutes

Cook time: 30 minutes

Total time: 45 minutes

Servings: 10

Calories: 292 KCAL

Ingredients:

- 1 large onion, chopped
- 2 cloves garlic minced
- 2 celery stalks, chopped
- 2 carrots, chopped
- 2 tablespoons of tomato paste
- 1 to 2 Mato peeled and chopped
- 4 tablespoons of arrowroot starch
- 6 cups of peeled and chopped butternut squash cut in 1" cubes
- ½ cup of Marsala wine
- 2 ½ cup of beef broth
- 3 tablespoons of extra virgin olive oil
- 2 bay leaves
- 1 teaspoon of sweet Hungarian paprika
- 1 teaspoon of thyme
- 1 teaspoon of rosemary

Cooking Instructions:

1. Press the Sauté function and add the olive oil.

2. Add the onions, garlic, celery, carrots, tomato and tomato paste to the pot. Generously season with salt and freshly ground black pepper.

3. Give everything a good stir. Season beef stew with salt, black pepper and 4 tablespoons of arrowroot starch (or cornstarch).

4. Add the beef and butternut squash into the bottom of your Instant Pot. Season butternut squash with salt and freshly ground black pepper.

5. Season everything with sweet Hungarian paprika, thyme, rosemary and add 2 bay leaves.

6. Pour wine and beef broth, and the rest of the 2 tablespoons of olive oil. Secure the lid in place and ensure that the valve is in sealing position.

7. Select Meat/Stew function to for 30 minutes. When the timer beeps, do a natural pressure release for about 15 minutes.

8. Serve and enjoy!

Cuban Shredded Beef Stew

Preparation time: 20 minutes

Cook time: 40 minutes

Total time: 1 hour

Serves: 6-8

- 1 tbsp. of olive oil
- 2 pounds of beef flank steak
- Salt & pepper to taste
- 1 medium onion, sliced
- 4-5 cloves garlic, minced
- 1 cup of beef or chicken broth
- 1 15 oz. can diced tomatoes
- 2 cups of sliced mild/sweet peppers of your choice
- ½ tsp. of dried oregano
- 1 tsp. of ground cumin
- 1 bay leaf
- ½ - 1 tsp. of Goya Sazon or Adobo seasoning
- ½ cup of chopped fresh parsley
- 2 tbsp. of vinegar (top choices: white wine, distilled, apple cider)
- ½ cup of chopped green olives

Cooking Instructions:

1. Generously season the flank steak on both sides with salt and pepper.

2. Press the Sauté setting and add the olive oil. Add the meat and cook to brown on both sides. Transfer the meat to a plate.

3. Add the onions and garlic to the pot, and sauté, stirring frequently, until the onions start to soften.

4. Add the broth and deglaze the pot to remove any browned bits that stuck to the bottom. Add the canned tomatoes, sliced peppers, oregano, cumin, and bay leaf and seasoning blend, if desired.

5. Add the browned flank steak into the stew and give everything a good stir. Secure the lid in place and ensure that the valve is in sealing position.

6. Select Manual High Pressure for 40 minutes. When the timer beeps, do a natural pressure release for about 10 minutes.

7. Carefully remove the lid and shred the meat with two forks. Discard the bay leaf. Mix in the parsley, vinegar and green olives. Season with salt and pepper to taste.

8. Serve with rice and enjoy!

Creamed Fennel and Cauliflower Soup

Serves: 4

Preparation time: 5 minutes

Cook time: 5 minutes

Total time: 10 minutes

Ingredients:

For the Salad:

- 1 tbsp. of coconut oil
- 1 white onion, sliced
- 3 cloves garlic, minced
- 1 large or 2 medium sized fennel bulbs, stalks and fronds removed, chopped
- 1 lb. of cauliflower florets
- 1 cup of coconut milk
- 3 cups of broth (bone broth or vegetable broth)
- 2 tsp. of salt
- Optional: Truffle oil, for serving
- Optional: Black pepper for serving

Cooking Instructions:

1. Press the Sauté function in your Instant Pot and add the coconut oil.

2. Add the onions and sauté until translucent. Add the garlic, fennel, and cauliflower. Cook for about 5 to 10 minutes, until the edges of the vegetables start to turn golden.

3. Add the broth, salt and coconut milk into the bottom of your Instant Pot. Secure the lid in place and ensure that the valve is in sealing position.

4. Select the Soup function for 5 minutes. When the timer beeps, do a quick pressure release. Carefully remove the lid.

5. Puree the soup with immersion blender until your desired creamy consistency is achieved.

6. Scoop into serving plates and drizzle with truffle oil. Top with freshly cracked pepper, and garnish with a leftover fennel frond.

7. Serve warm and enjoy!

Hearty Beef Stew

Preparation time: 10 minutes

Cook time: 35 minutes

Total time: 45 minutes

Ingredients:

- 1 pound of stew meat
- 2 cups of beef stock
- 1 onion (chopped)
- 3 Yukon gold potatoes, chopped
- 1 cup of carrots, chopped
- 1 tablespoon of oil
- Salt and pepper to taste
- 1 teaspoon of garlic powder
- 1 teaspoon of paprika
- 2 tablespoons of flour
- 1 tablespoon of tomato paste

Ingredients:

1. Press the Sauté function on your Instant Pot and add the oil.

2. Add the meat and cook until the meat is no longer pink. Add the chopped vegetables and give everything a good stir to combine.

3. Add the broth and seasonings. Stir again and secure the lid in place. Select Stew/Meat" function to cook for 35 minutes.

4. When the timer beeps, do a quick pressure release. Ladle out ¼ of your liquid and combine it with your flour to create a slurry.

5. Add the slurry back into your stew and give everything a good stir to combine. Adjust seasoning with salt and pepper to taste.

6. Serve warm and enjoy!

CHICKEN

Honey Teriyaki Chicken

Preparation time: 10 minutes

Cook time: 35 minutes

Total time: 45 minutes

Ingredients:

- 4 boneless skinless chicken breasts (or 6 chicken thighs)
- 1 1/3 cup soy sauce
- ½ cup of water
- 2/3 cup honey
- 2 tsp. of minced garlic
- ½ cup rice vinegar
- ½ tsp. of ground ginger
- ¼ - ½ tsp. of crushed red pepper flakes use ½ tsp. for a more noticeable touch of heat
- 3 tbsp. of corn starch + 3 tbsp. of cold water
- 2 tsp. sesame seeds
- Diced green onions, for topping
- Steamed white rice or fried rice, for serving

Cooking Instructions:

1. Add the chicken into the bottom of your Instant Pot.

2. In a medium bowl, whisk together soy sauce, water, honey, garlic, rice vinegar, ground ginger, and crushed red pepper flakes.

3. Pour the mixture over chicken. Secure the lid in place and ensure that the valve is in sealing position.

4. Select Manual High Pressure for 35 minutes for frozen chicken, 30 minutes for thawed. When the timer beeps, do a natural pressure release.

5. Carefully open the lid and shred the chicken with two forks. Remove any pieces of fat from your Instant Pot with a slotted spoon.

6. Select the Soup function and once liquid comes to a boil, stir together corn starch and water. Whisk into the sauce until thickened.

7. Stir in sesame seeds. Turn off your Instant Pot and add the shredded chicken back to the pot. Give everything a good stir to coat in the sauce. Garnish with chopped green onions.

8. Serve over steamed or fried rice and enjoy!

BBQ Chicken Sliders

Preparation time: 10 minutes

Cook time: 15 minutes

Total time: 25 minutes

Ingredients:

- 12 slider buns
- 4 frozen chicken breasts
- 2 cups of your favorite BBQ sauce

Cooking Instructions:

1. Add the chicken breast into the bottom of you Instant Pot.

2. Pour 1 cup of water. Secure the lid in place and ensure that the valve is in sealing position.

3. Select Manual High Pressure for 15 minutes. When the timer beeps, do a natural pressure release.

4. Carefully remove the lid and drain off any water. Shred the chicken with two forks.

5. Stir in BBQ sauce.

6. Serve on slider buns with your desired toppings.

Teriyaki Rice with Chicken & Vegetables

Preparation time: 8 minutes

Cook time: 22 minutes

Total time: 32 minutes

Servings: 4

Ingredients:

For the Teriyaki sauce

- 1/3 cup low sodium soy sauce can also use gluten free tamari or coconut amino
- ¼ cup of rice wine vinegar or apple cider vinegar
- ¼ cup of honey
- 1 ½ tbsp. of Mirin or dry sherry, optional
- 1 tsp. of arrowroot starch or corn starch
- 3 tbsp. of water plus more as needed to thin out sauce

For the Rice and Chicken:

- 1 ½ tbsp. of toasted sesame oil or olive oil
- 1 medium boneless skinless chicken breast cut into cubes
- Salt and black pepper to taste
- 2 garlic cloves, minced
- ½ tsp. of grated or minced ginger
- 1/3 cup of chopped red bell peppers
- 1/3 cup of shredded carrots
- 1 ½ cups of uncooked Jasmine rice washed, rinsed and drained thoroughly
- 1 ¼ cups of water
- ½ - 1 cup broccoli florets
- 1/3 cup of frozen shelled Edamame beans thawed
- Sesame seeds for garnish
- Chopped green onions for garnish

Cooking Instructions:

1. Press the Sauté function on your Instant Pot and add the oil.

2. Add the chicken and season with salt and pepper. In a medium bowl, whisk together the soy sauce, vinegar, honey and Mirin.

3. Sauté for 2-3 minutes, until lightly brown. Add the garlic and ginger and sauté for additional 20 seconds.

4. Add in half of the sauce, the uncooked rice and 1 cup of water. Secure the lid in place and ensure that the valve is in sealing position.

5. Select Manual High Pressure for 3 minutes. When the timer beeps, do a natural pressure release for about 10 minutes.

6. Carefully open the lid and press the Sauté function. Add the bell peppers, carrots, broccoli and edamame.

7. Whisk the cornstarch slurry together with the reserved amount of sauce and drizzle into your pot.

8. Cook until vegetables are tender. Sprinkle with sesame seeds and green onions, if desired.

9. Serve warm and enjoy!

Chicken Paprika

Preparation time: 10 minutes

Cook time: 13 minutes

Total time: 23 minutes

Servings: 4

Calories: 569 kcal

Ingredients:

- 1 large onion, diced
- 2 garlic cloves, minced
- 3 tablespoons of olive oil
- 2 pounds of skinless chicken thighs, bone in (900g)
- 1 teaspoon of salt
- ¼ teaspoon of black pepper
- 2 tablespoons of sweet paprika
- 1 bay leaf
- 1½ cup of chicken stock
- 1 cup of heavy cream
- 2 tablespoons of sour cream
- 5 tablespoons of corn starch
- ½ lemon or more to taste

Cooking Instructions:

1. Press "Sauté" button on your Instant Pot and add 3 tbsp. of olive oil.

2. Add the onion and garlic. Sauté the contents for a couple of minutes, stirring frequently. Add the chicken thighs. Cook them on both each side for some minutes.

3. Add salt, pepper and sweet paprika. Give everything a good stir to coat with the seasoning. Throw in bay leaf and pour in the chicken stock.

4. Secure the lid in place and ensure that the valve is in sealing position. Select Manual High Pressure for 5 minutes. When the timer beeps, do a natural pressure release for about 10 minutes. Carefully open the lid.

5. Press "Sauté" function and pour in heavy cream, sour cream and corn starch diluted in little water. Squeeze in the juice of ½ lemon and taste. Add more seasoning or lemon juice, if desired.

6. Serve with dumplings, or your desired pasta and enjoy!

Faux-Tisserie Chicken

Preparation time: 5 minutes

Cook time: 33 minutes

Total time: 38 minutes

Servings: 4

Calories: 443 kcal

Ingredients:

- 3 lb. whole chicken
- 2 tbsp. of olive oil (divided)
- Sea salt & black pepper, to taste
- ½ medium onion, cut into quarters
- 5 large cloves fresh garlic, peeled and left whole
- 1 cup chicken stock/broth, or water

Southwest Seasoning:

- 1 tsp. of garlic powder
- 1 tsp. of onion powder
- 1 tsp. of chili powder
- ½ tsp. of cumin
- ½ tsp. of basil

Cooking Instructions:

1. Season the chicken with 1 tbsp. of olive oil. Sprinkle with salt and pepper.

2. Add the onion wedges and garlic cloves inside the chicken. Secure the legs with butcher's twine.

3. Press the Sauté function and add the remaining oil. When hot, add the chicken and brown both sides, about 4 minutes.

4. Remove the chicken and set aside. Add the trivet into the bottom of your Instant Pot and add the chicken stock.

5. Sprinkle seasoning mix over the chicken, rubbing it in and spreading it around to coat the entire chicken.

6. Add the chicken, breast side up on top of the trivet. Secure the lid in place and ensure that the valve is in sealing position.

7. Select Manual High Pressure for 25 minutes. When the time is up, do a natural pressure release for about 15 minutes.

8. Carefully remove the lid and remove the chicken. Let the chicken rest for about 7 minutes before serving.

9. Serve and enjoy!

Cajun Chicken and Rice

Preparation time: 10 minutes

Cook time: 20 minutes

Total time: 30 minutes

Servings: 4 -5 servings

Calories: 473 kcal

Ingredients:

- 1 pound of chicken breast
- 1 tbsp. of Cajun seasoning, divided
- 1 tbsp. of oil olive or avocado
- 1 small onion, diced
- 3 garlic cloves, minced
- 1.5 cups of white rice (we used regular white, Jasmine and parboiled rice with success) well rinsed
- 1 bell pepper, diced (we used 1 to 2 cups of frozen peas, carrots and corn instead)
- 1 tbsp. of tomato paste
- 1.75 cups of chicken or vegetable broth

Cooking Instructions:

1. First, rinse the rice until the water runs clear. Cut the chicken breasts in half lengthwise to make them thinner.

2. Season the chicken on both sides with Cajun seasoning (about 2 tsp.). Press the Sauté function on your Instant Pot and add the oil.

3. Sauté the onion and garlic with. Deglaze the pot with water to remove any browned pit stuck to the pot.

4. Add rice, bell peppers, tomato paste and 1 tsp of Cajun seasoning into the bottom of your Instant Pot. Give everything a good stir to combine.

5. Pour the broth over the rice mixture and carefully arrange the chicken breast halves over top.

6. Secure the lid in place and ensure that the valve is in sealing position. Select Manual High Pressure for 8 minutes.

7. When the timer beeps, do a natural pressure release for about 5 minutes, then release any remaining pressure.

8. Carefully remove the lid and shred the chicken with two forks. Add the chicken back into the pot and stir to combine.

9. Adjust seasoning to taste with more salt and pepper.

10. Serve with chopped cilantro and a squeeze of lime juice.

Chicken Pho

Preparation time: 10 minutes

Cook time: 30 minutes

Total time: 40 minutes

Servings: 4

Calories: 842 KCAL

Ingredients:

- 14 ounces rice noodles
- 1 tablespoon of olive oil extra virgin
- 1 large yellow onion, halved
- 1 2-inch piece ginger cut into ¼ inch slices and slightly smashed
- 3 cardamom pods lightly smashed
- 1 cinnamon stick
- 1 tablespoon of coriander seeds
- 3 star anise pods
- 5 cloves
- 1 fuji apple peeled, cored and cut into ½ chunks
- ½ cup coarsely chopped cilantro leaves
- 6 chicken thighs bone-in, skin-on
- 3 tablespoons of fish sauce
- 1 tablespoon of sugar
- 8 cups of water
- 1 ½ teaspoon of kosher salt

Toppings:

- 1 lime cut into wedges
- 2 jalapenos, thinly sliced
- ½ red onion, thinly sliced and soaked in cold water for 10 minutes
- Fresh herbs (mint, cilantro, basil)
- Bean sprouts
- Sriracha sauce
- Daikon radish sprouts (optional)

Cooking Instructions:

1. In a medium bowl, soak the noodles with warm water for about 30 to 45 minutes.

2. Press the Sauté function on your Instant Pot and add the oil. Ass the onion and ginger. Cook, without stirring, for about 4 minutes, until slightly charred.

3. Add the cardamom, cinnamon stick, coriander, star anise and cloves and sauté for additional 1 minute until fragrant.

4. Add the water into the bottom of your Instant Pot with apple, cilantro, chicken, fish sauce, and sugar.

5. Secure the lid in place and ensure that the valve is in sealing position. Select Manual High Pressure for 15 minutes.

6. When the timer beeps, do a natural pressure release for about 10 minutes, the quick release any remaining pressure. Carefully open the lid and remove chicken from the pot.

7. Strain the broth and season with salt and pepper, to taste. Skim some of the fat from the broth. Shred the chicken with two forks and add them back to your pot.

8. Strain the noodles and divide them among the 4 bowls. Top each of the bowls with the broth and your favorite toppings.

9. Serve and enjoy!

Butter Chicken

Preparation time: 10 minutes

Cook time: 5 minutes

Total time: 15 minutes

Servings: 6

Calories: 574 kcal

Ingredients:

- 6 chicken thighs boneless, skinless, cut into cubes
- 1 ½ cup of heavy cream
- 1 ½ cup of tomato sauce
- ½ onion, chopped
- 5 tablespoons of butter
- 1 tablespoon of minced garlic
- 1 tablespoon of chopped ginger
- 1 ½ teaspoon of chili powder
- 1 ½ teaspoon of cumin
- 3 teaspoons of garam masala
- 2 tablespoons of corn starch, optional

Cooking Instructions:

1. Press the Sauté function on your Instant Pot and add the butter.

2. When butter is melted, add the cubed chicken and onion. Sauté until the chicken pieces are cooked through. Add all the remaining ingredients into your Instant Pot.

3. Give everything a good mix. Secure the lid in place and ensure that the valve is in sealing position. Select Manual High Pressure for 5 minutes.

4. When the timer beeps, do a natural pressure release. Carefully open the lid and remove the chicken from the pot.

5. Shred the chicken with two forks and add back to the pot. In a medium bowl, add some hot liquid with 1 tablespoon of cornstarch and whisk together.

6. Add the mixture into the pot and give everything a good stir. The mixture will thicken the sauce as it cools.

7. Serve with rice and/or naan and enjoy!

Spicy Honey Chicken

Preparation time: 15 minutes

Cook time: 4 minutes

Total time: 19 minutes

Servings: 6

Calories: 155 kcal

Ingredients:

- 4 chicken breasts cut into bite size chunks
- 1 tablespoon of brown sugar
- 3 tablespoons of honey
- 1 tablespoon of minced ginger
- 1.5 tablespoon of minced garlic
- ¼ cup of soy sauce
- 1 tablespoon of Sriracha
- 1 teaspoon of Worcestershire sauce
- ½ onion, sliced or diced
- 1 tablespoon of sesame seeds, optional
- 2 green onions, optional
- 2 tablespoons of cornstarch

Cooking Instructions:

1. First, cut the chicken breasts into large bite size chunks. Cut the onion into chunks.

2. Add the chicken and onions into the bottom of your Instant Pot. In a medium bowl, mix together the remaining ingredients (except the cornstarch) with a fork.

3. Pour the mixture over the chicken. Secure the lid in place and ensure that the valve is in sealing position.

4. Select Manual High Pressure for 4 minutes. When the timer beeps, do a quick pressure release.

5. Carefully remove the lid. In a medium bowl, add some of the hot sauce with the cornstarch and whisk together. Add the mixture into the pot.

6. Press the Sauté function and allow to bubble for a couple of minutes. Let to sit for a couple of minutes to thicken the sauce.

7. Serve spicy honey chicken over rice.

Salsa Chicken Tacos

Preparation time: 10 minutes

Cook time: 25 minutes

Total time: 35 minutes

Servings: 5

Ingredients:

- 1 ½ pounds of boneless skinless chicken breasts
- 2 teaspoons of ancho chili powder
- 1 teaspoon of ground cumin
- ½ teaspoon of ground coriander
- Salt and freshly ground black pepper
- 1 clove garlic, minced
- 1 cup of fire roasted jarred salsa
- 2 tablespoons of chopped cilantro
- For serving: 10 corn or flour tortilla shells warmed, Shredded Monterey jack or Mexican blend cheese, Shredded romaine lettuce, Diced roma tomatoes, Guacamole or diced avocados and Sour cream and hot sauce optional

Cooking Instructions:

1. In a medium bowl, whisk together the chili powder, cumin, coriander and ¼ teaspoon of salt and ¼ teaspoon of pepper.

2. Sprinkle the mixture over the chicken and sprinkle garlic over chicken. Pour the salsa over chicken to cover.

3. Secure the lid in place and ensure that the valve is in sealing position. Select Poultry function to cook for 13 minutes.

4. When the timer beeps, do a natural pressure release. Carefully open the lid and shred the chicken with two forks.

5. Sprinkle in cilantro, and toss chicken to coat. Season with more salt to taste if desired. Add in tortilla shells with your desired toppings.

6. Serve and enjoy!

FISH & SEAFOODS
Easy Coconut Red Curry Shrimp

Preparation time: 5 minutes

Cook time: 30 minutes

Total time: 35 minutes

Servings: 6

Ingredients:

For The Marinade:

- ¼ cup of coconut milk canned
- 1 teaspoon of cumin
- 1 teaspoon of paprika
- 2 teaspoon of curry spice
- 3 tablespoons of fresh lime juice
- ½ teaspoon of sea salt
- 1 teaspoon of freshly grated ginger
- 1 clove garlic, minced
- 2 pounds of large shrimp peeled and deveined

For The Sauce:

- 2 tablespoons of coconut oil or olive oil
- 1 small white onion, diced
- 2 teaspoons of freshly grated ginger
- 2 cloves garlic, minced
- 1 28 ounces can of diced tomatoes
- 3 tablespoons of red Thai curry paste
- 1 14 ounces coconut milk
- 1 teaspoon of sea salt
- 1/3 cup of freshly chopped cilantro for garnish, optional

Cooking Instructions:

1. Prepare the marinade. In a medium bowl, add the coconut milk, spices, lime juice, sea salt, ginger, and garlic.

2. Whisk together, then add shrimp. Toss everything to coat and allow to sit for a couple minutes.

3. Press the Sauté function on your Instant Pot and add the oil. Add the onion, ginger, and garlic. Cook for a couple of minutes and select Cancel.

4. Add tomatoes, curry paste, coconut milk, and salt. Secure the lid in place and ensure that the valve is in sealing position.

5. Select Manual High Pressure for 7 minutes. When the timer beeps, do a quick pressure release.

6. Carefully open the lid. Select Sauté function and add in shrimp plus juices from the marinade.

7. Simmer for about 2 to 3 minutes or until the shrimp is cooked through and no longer pink.

8. Serve with optional cilantro, salt to taste, and over rice or cauliflower rice.

Steamed Alaskan Crab Legs

Preparation time: 10 minutes

Cook time: 4 minutes

Total time: 14 minutes

Ingredients:

- 2-3 lbs. of frozen crab legs
- 1 cup of water
- ½ tbsp. of salt
- Melted butter for serving

Cooking Instructions:

1. Add steamer basket into the bottom of your Instant Pot. Pour 1 cup of water and ½ tbsp. of salt.

2. Add half of the Alaskan King Crab Legs along with 1 tbsp. of salt.

3. Secure the lid in place and ensure that the valve is in sealing position.

4. Select Manual High Pressure for 4 minutes. When the timer beeps, do a natural pressure release.

5. Carefully open the lid and remove the crab legs. Shred the crab legs and add back to the pot. Give everything a good stir.

6. Serve with melted butter. Repeat process with remaining half of crab legs.

10-Minute Instant Pot Salmon

Serves: 4

Preparation time: 10 minutes

Cook time: 5 minutes

Total time: 15 minutes

Ingredients:

- 3 medium, lemon
- ¾ cup, water
- 4 fillet, salmon
- 1 bunch dill weed, fresh
- 1 tbsp. of butter, unsalted
- ¼ tsp. of salt
- ¼ tsp. of black pepper, ground
- 1 cup brown rice, raw (Optional)
- 4 cup green beans (Optional)

Cooking Instructions:

1. Add fresh lemon juice and water into the bottom of your Instant Pot.

2. Place the steamer insert. Add the salmon fillets, frozen, on top of the steamer insert.

3. Sprinkle fresh dill on top of the salmon and add one slice of fresh lemon on top of each one.

4. Secure the lid in place and ensure that the valve is in sealing position. Select Manual High Pressure for 5 minutes.

5. When the timer beeps, do a quick pressure release. Carefully remove the lid and season with salt and pepper to taste.

6. Serve with butter, extra dill and lemon.

Shrimp and Lentil Stew

Preparation time: 10 minutes

Cook time: 12 minutes

Total time: 22 minutes

Servings: 6

Ingredients:

- 1 tbsp. of olive oil
- 3 cloves garlic, minced
- 1 onion, chopped small
- 1 red bell pepper, chopped
- 1 tbsp. of thyme
- 2 tsp. of oregano
- 2 tsp. of Old Bay Seasoning
- ½ tsp. of cayenne
- 1 cup of lentils
- 1 pound shrimp, deveined and peeled
- 3 cups of chicken broth (or vegetable)
- 1 15 ounces can diced tomatoes, drain slightly
- ½ cup tomato sauce
- 2 tbsp. of Worcestershire sauce
- 1 cup frozen riced broccoli

Cooking Instructions:

1. Press the Sauté function and add the olive oil. Add the garlic, onion, and bell pepper and cook for about 5 minutes, or until ingredients are softened.

2. Add the thyme, oregano, Old Bay, and cayenne and give everything a good toss to mix. Cook the contents for more 1 minute.

3. Add the lentils, shrimp, chicken broth, diced tomatoes, tomato sauce, Worcestershire sauce and riced broccoli into the bottom of your Instant Pot.

4. Secure the lid in place and ensure that the valve is in sealing position. Select Manual High Pressure for 12 minutes.

5. When the timer beeps, do a natural pressure release. Carefully remove the lid and season with salt and pepper.

6. Serve and enjoy!

Bang Bang Shrimp Pasta

Serving: 6

Preparation time: 5 minutes

Cook time: 6 minutes

Total time: 11 minutes

Ingredients:

- 1 lb. of dried spaghetti
- 3 cloves garlic, minced
- 1 tsp. of coconut oil
- 4 ¼ cup of water
- 1 lb. of raw deveined jumbo shrimp
- ¾ cup of light mayonnaise
- ¾ cup of Thai sweet chili sauce
- ¼ cup of lime juice
- 1+ tbsp. of Sriracha sauce
- ½ cup of chopped scallions
- Salt and pepper

Cooking Instructions:

1. First, break up the spaghetti noodles in half and add them in the Instant Pot.

2. Add the garlic, coconut oil, 1 tsp. of salt, and water. Secure the lid in place and ensure that the valve is in sealing position.

3. Select Manual High Pressure for 4 minutes. When the timer beeps, do a quick pressure release.

4. In a medium bowl, mix together the mayonnaise, Thai sweet chili sauce, lime juice, and Sriracha together. Carefully open the lid and stir the sauce into the pasta.

5. Pour in the shrimp and scallions and give everything a good stir to combine. Press the Sauté function and cook for about 2 to 3 minutes.

6. Simmer until the shrimp are pink. Season with salt and pepper as needed. Add more Sriracha if desired.

7. Serve hot and enjoy!

Creamy Chipotle Shrimp Soup

Preparation time: 5 minutes

Cook time: 25 minutes

Total time: 30 minutes

Servings: 5

Ingredients:

- 3 slices bacon, chopped
- 1 cup onion, diced
- ¾ cup of celery, chopped
- 1 teaspoon of garlic
- 1 tablespoon of flour
- ¼ cup of dry white wine
- 1 ½ cups of chicken or vegetable broth
- ½ cup of whole milk
- 1 ½ cups potatoes, cut into small (1/3-inch) cubes
- 1 cup of frozen corn kernels
- 2 teaspoons of diced canned chipotle peppers in adobo sauce
- ¾ teaspoon of salt (or to taste)
- ½ teaspoon of ground black pepper
- ½ teaspoon of dried thyme
- ½ pound shrimp, peeled and deveined
- ¼ cup of heavy cream

Cooking Instructions:

1. Press the 'Sauté' setting and add bacon to inner pot of your Instant Pot.

2. Cook, stirring frequently for about 3 minutes or until crisp. Add onions, celery and garlic. Sauté until vegetables have softened. Stir in flour and sauté for 1 minute.

3. Deglaze the pot with white wine to scrape any browned bit stuck to the pot. Stir in broth, milk, potatoes, corn, Chipotle, salt, black pepper and thyme.

4. Secure the lid in place and ensure that the valve is in sealing position. Select Manual High Pressure for 1 minute. Do a Quick Release of Pressure

5. Carefully open the lid and stir in shrimp and cream. Secure the lid in place and let the shrimp cook in the residual heat for 10 minutes.

6. Garnish with scallions, parsley and/or crumbled bacon and serve immediately.

Alaskan Cod with Fennel, Olives and Potatoes

Servings: 2

Preparation time: 15 minutes

Cook time: 25 minutes

Total time: 40 minutes

Ingredients:

- 2 tbsp. of olive oil
- ½ medium onion, halved
- 1 head garlic, halved
- 1½ cups of chicken stock
- ¼ cup of olive brine
- ¼ cup of canned tomato purée
- Salt and pepper, to taste
- ½ cup of green olives, pitted and crushed
- 1 head fennel, quartered
- 1 medium russet potato, cut into 6 pieces
- 1 12-ounce Alaskan cod fillet, cut into 3-inch blocks
- ¼ bunch basil, leaves torn
- 1 lemon, sliced, for garnish

Cooking Instructions:

1. Press the Sauté function on your Instant Pot and add the olive oil when hot.

2. Add the onion and garlic halves cut-sides down. Sauté them for about 3 minutes or until caramelized.

3. Add the stock, olive brine and tomato purée. Turn off the Sauté setting. Season the broth with salt and pepper.

4. Add the olives, fennel and potatoes to the broth. Secure the lid in place and ensure that the valve is in sealing position.

5. Cook on Low Pressure for 10 minutes. When the timer beeps, do a quick pressure release. Carefully open the lid and remove all the vegetables with a slotted spoon.

6. Leave the broth in the pot. Season the cod with salt and pepper, and add the pieces into the broth.

7. Secure the lid in place and ensure that the valve is in sealing position. Cook on Low Pressure for 4 minutes. When the timer beeps, do a quick pressure release.

8. Carefully open the lid and remove the fish with a slotted spoon. Add the torn basil to broth. Fill a bowl with the fish and vegetables, and spoon the broth over the top.

9. Serve with a slice of lemon.

Lemon Pepper Salmon

Preparation time: 5 minutes

Cook time: 10 minutes

Total time: 15 minutes

Servings: 3 -4

Calories: 296 KCAL

Ingredients:

- ¾ cup of water
- A few sprigs of parsley dill, tarragon, basil or a combo
- 1 lb. salmon filet skin on
- 3 tsp. of ghee or other healthy fat divided
- ¼ tsp. of salt or to taste
- ½ tsp. of pepper or to taste
- ½ lemon, thinly sliced
- 1 zucchini julienned
- 1 red bell pepper julienned
- 1 carrot julienned

Cooking Instructions:

1. Add water and herbs into the bottom of your Instant Pot and place the steamer rack.

2. Add the salmon, skin down on rack. Drizzle salmon with ghee/fat, season with salt and pepper, and cover with lemon slices.

3. Secure the lid in place and ensure that the valve is in sealing position. Select the Steam function for 3 minutes. While salmon cooks, julienne your veggies.

4. When the timer beeps, do a quick pressure release. Carefully open the lid and remove rack with salmon. Remove herbs and discard. Add veggies and secure the lid in place.

5. Press "Sauté" setting and allow the veggies to cook for about 2 minutes. Add the remaining teaspoon of fat and give everything a good stir.

6. Serve with salmon and enjoy!

Fish and Corn Chowder

Servings: 4

Preparation time: 5 minutes

Cook time: 5 minutes

Total time: 10 minutes

Ingredients:

- ¾ cup chopped bacon
- 1 medium onion, chopped
- 2 ribs celery, chopped
- 1 medium carrot, chopped
- 2 cloves garlic, minced or pressed
- 3 cups peeled & cubed potatoes preferably Yukon gold
- 4 cups of chicken bone-broth or vegetable broth
- 2 tbsp. of butter (pasture raised, grass fed) or ghee
- 1 lb. wild caught Haddock Filets FROZEN
- 1 cup of frozen or freeze-dried corn
- Sea salt (real salt)
- Ground white pepper
- 2 cups of organic heavy cream
- 1 heaping tbsp. of organic potato starch

Cooking Instructions:

1. Press the Sauté function on your Instant Pot and cook bacon in butter until crispy.

2. Add the onion, garlic, carrot and celery. Sauté for about 3 minutes or until veggies are soft. Season with sea salt and white pepper.

3. Add potatoes, corn, fish and broth. Secure the lid in place and ensure that the valve is in sealing position.

4. Select Manual High Pressure for 5 minutes. When the timer beeps, do a natural pressure release. In a medium bowl, combine together the heavy cream and potato starch.

5. Add the mixture to chowder and give everything a good stir. Press the Warm function and allow it to thicken slightly for about 2-3 minutes.

6. Serve and enjoy!

Lobster Bisque

Preparation time: 6 minutes

Cook time: 4 minutes

Total time: 10 minutes

Ingredients:

- 1 cup of diced carrots
- 1 cup of diced celery
- 29 ounces canned petite diced tomatoes
- 2 whole shallots, minced
- 1 clove garlic, minced
- 1 tablespoon of butter
- 32 ounces low-sodium chicken broth
- 1 tablespoon of Old Bay Seasoning
- 1 teaspoon of dried dill
- 1 teaspoon of freshly ground black pepper
- 5 teaspoons of paprika
- 4 lobster tails (or 24 ounces frozen lobster)

Cooking Instructions:

1. In a microwave safe bowl, add the butter, minced shallots and garlic.

2. Microwave on high for about 2 to 3 minutes, or until shallots and garlic are translucent.

3. Add the tomatoes, carrots, celery, minced shallots and garlic into the bottom of your Instant Pot. Add chicken broth and spices.

4. Cut off the fan at the end of the lobster and add them into the pot. Secure the lid in place. Select Manual High Pressure for 4 minutes.

5. When the timer beeps, do a natural pressure release. Carefully open the lid and puree the soup mixture with an immersion blender to your desired consistency.

6. Add the cream and give everything a good stir.

7. Serve and enjoy!

TURKEY

Turkey Meatball & Ditalini Soup

Preparation time: 10 minutes

Cook time: 15 minutes

Total time: 30 minutes

Ingredients:

For the Meatballs:

- 1 lb. 93% lean ground turkey
- 1/3 cup of seasoned breadcrumbs (Can substitute gluten-free breadcrumbs)
- 3 tablespoons of grated Pecorino Romano cheese
- 1 large egg, beaten
- 1 clove crushed garlic
- 1 tablespoon of fresh minced parsley
- ½ tsp. of kosher salt

Soup Ingredients:

- Cooking spray
- 1 tsp. of olive oil
- ½ cup of chopped onion
- ½ cup of chopped celery
- ½ cup of chopped carrot
- 3 cloves minced garlic
- 1 can (28 oz.) diced San Marzano tomatoes, we used Tuttorosso
- 4 cups of reduced sodium chicken broth
- 4 torn basil leaves, plus optional more for garnish
- 2 bay leaves
- 5 oz. ditalini pasta (1 cup) (wheat or gluten-free)
- 1 cup of zucchini, diced small
- Parmesan rind, optional
- Grated parmesan cheese, optional for serving

Cooking Instructions:

1. In a medium bowl, combine together the turkey, breadcrumbs, pecorino, egg, garlic, parsley and salt and give everything a good mix to combine.

2. Form into 30 meatballs, about 1 heaping tablespoon each. Remove the meatballs and set aside. Set your Instant Pot to Sauté function and spray with oil.

3. Brown the meatballs in 2 to 3 batches, spraying each time. Add oil and sauté the onion, celery, carrots and garlic until soft for about 4 minutes.

4. Add the tomatoes, Parmesan rind, basil, bay leaves and give everything a god stir. Add the meatballs back to the pot.

5. Add the chicken broth and secure the lid in place. Select Manual High Pressure for 15 minutes. When the timer beeps, do a quick pressure release.

6. Carefully remove the lid and add the pasta and zucchini. Cook for about 4 minutes and do a quick pressure release to avoid overcooking the pasta.

7. Serve with grated cheese if desired and basil.

Pumpkin Turkey Chile Mole

Preparation time: 10 minutes

Cook time: 40 minutes

Total time: 50 minutes

Serves: 6

Ingredients:

- 1 pound of ground turkey
- 1 tablespoon of ghee
- 1 medium yellow onion, chopped
- 1 bell pepper, chopped
- 3 tablespoons of minced garlic
- 2 tablespoons of cocoa powder
- 1 ½ tablespoon of ancho chile powder
- 1 teaspoon of cinnamon
- ½ teaspoon of ground cloves
- 1 cup of filtered water
- 4 Scoops Vital Proteins Chicken Bone Broth Collagen
- 1 28 ounces can diced tomatoes
- 1 can pumpkin
- 1 can tomato paste (5 ounces)
- 2 teaspoons of sea salt, divided
- Fresh ground black pepper, to taste
- For serving: Pumpkin seeds, Chopped cilantro, Sliced avocado, Coconut cream or coconut milk yogurt

Cooking Instructions:

1. Press the "Sauté" function on your Instant Pot and add 1 tablespoon of ghee when hot.

2. Add the onion, pepper, and a pinch of salt. Cook for about 3 to 4 minutes, or until the vegetables start to soften.

3. Stir in the tomato paste and garlic, and sauté for about 30 seconds, or until fragrant. Add in the turkey and 1 ½ teaspoon of sea salt.

4. Sauté the turkey for a couple a minutes to brown. Add the spices (ancho chili powder, cinnamon, and cloves, cocoa).

5. Add the diced tomatoes, 1 cup of water, 4 scoops of vital proteins collagen, and the can of pumpkin.

6. Secure the lid in place and ensure that the valve is in sealing position. Select Manual High Pressure for 15 minutes.

7. When the timer beeps, do a quick pressure release. Press the Sauté setting and allow to cook for about 5 minutes.

8. Garnish with some avocado slices, chopped cilantro, and pumpkin seeds.

9. Serve and enjoy!

Italian Turkey Stuffed Sweet Potatoes

Ingredients:

- 1.5 cups of water
- 2 sweet potatoes of very similar size
- 0.75 pound ground Italian turkey or chicken
- ½ cup of sliced sweet yellow onion
- 2 tbsp. of avocado oil
- 4 cups of spinach, optional
- Optional garnish: parsley red pepper, and cheeses

Cooking Instructions:

1. Pour 1.5 cups of water into the bottom of your Instant Pot.

2. Add the washed sweet potatoes on top of the rack and place into your Instant Pot. Once your sweet potatoes are done, release the pressure.

3. Carefully open the lid and remove the sweet potatoes and drain the instant pot. Press the Sauté function on your Instant Pot and add the oil.

4. Add the onions and sauté until translucent and tender. Add the ground meat and cook until cooked through.

5. Once the meat is done, add in 4 cups of spinach and sauté until wilted.

6. Cut your sweet potatoes in half and mush the center down with a fork to fill them with meat filling. Garnish with parsley, red pepper and cheese if desired.

7. Serve and enjoy!

Turkey Chili

Preparation time: 10 minutes

Cook time: 20 minutes

Total time: 30 minutes

Serves: 4

Ingredients:

- 2 tbsp. of olive oil
- 1 lb. of ground turkey
- 1 medium onion, finely diced
- 1 medium green bell pepper, cored and finely diced
- 3 medium carrots, peeled and thinly sliced
- 3 stalks celery, thinly sliced
- 3 cloves garlic, minced
- 1 (28 oz.) can crushed tomatoes
- 1 (15 oz.) can black beans, drained and rinsed
- 1 (4 oz.) can chopped green chili, drained
- ½ cup of water
- 3 tbsp. of chili powder
- 1 ½ tsp. ground cumin
- 1 tsp. of kosher salt
- 1 tsp. of tamari or soy sauce (optional)
- Toppings for serving: shredded cheddar cheese, sliced scallions, diced avocado, sour cream

Cooking Instructions:

1. Turn the Sauté function on and add the oil.

2. Add the turkey and cook, stirring frequently for about 4 minutes to break up the meat into small pieces, until no longer pink.

3. Add the onion, bell pepper, carrots, celery, and garlic. Stir and cook for 3 minutes. Add the tomatoes and black beans.

4. Add the green chili, water, chili powder, cumin, salt, and tamari or soy sauce if desired. Give everything a good stir to combine.

5. Secure the lid in place and ensure that the valve is in sealing position. Select Manual High Pressure for 20 minutes.

6. When the timer beeps, do a quick pressure release. Carefully remove the lid and stir the chili.

7. Add salt, soy sauce or tamari, and other seasonings as required. Give everything a good stir.

8. Serve with your desired toppings and enjoy!

Turkey Vegetable Lasagna Soup

Preparation time: 10 minutes

Cook time: 14 minutes

Total time: 24 minutes

Ingredients:

For the Soup:

- 1-2 tbsp. of olive oil
- 1 onion, diced
- 1 large carrot, peeled and diced
- 1 pound of ground turkey
- 2 cloves garlic, minced
- 1 tbsp. of Italian seasoning
- ½ tsp. of salt
- ½ tsp. of pepper
- 1 14.5 ounces can diced tomatoes
- 2 tbsp. of tomato paste
- 1 26 ounces jar spaghetti sauce (we used Trader Joe's Tomato Basil Sauce)
- 3 cups of chicken stock
- 2 small or 1 large zucchini, diced
- 6 ounces gluten-free lasagna noodles
- 1 cup of mozzarella cheese, grated
- 1 cup of spinach, chopped

For the Cheese Mixture:

- 1 cup of ricotta cheese
- ¼ cup of parmesan cheese
- ¼ tsp. of salt

Cooking Instructions:

1. Press the Sauté function on your Instant Pot and add the olive oil.

2. Add the onion and carrot. Sauté for about 3 minutes or until the vegetables begin to soften.

3. Add the ground turkey and sauté, breaking into small pieces with a spoon, until no longer pink.

4. Add the garlic, Italian seasoning, salt and pepper. Add the diced tomatoes, tomato paste, spaghetti sauce, and chicken stock and give everything a good stir to combine.

5. Break the lasagna noodles in half and add to the pot along with the zucchini. Secure the lid in place and ensure that the valve is in sealing position.

6. Select Manual High Pressure for 14 minutes. When the timer beeps, do a quick pressure release. Carefully open the lid and stir in the mozzarella and spinach.

7. In a medium bowl, combine together the ricotta, parmesan and salt. Give everything a good stir to combine.

8. Serve with a dollop of the cheese mixture and enjoy!

Turkey-Stuffed Peppers

Preparation time: 10 minutes

Cook time: 15 minutes

Total time: 25 minutes

Ingredients:

- 4 large multicolored bell peppers, tops cut off and chopped, peppers hollowed and seeded
- 1 lb. of 93% lean ground turkey
- ¾ cup of cooked brown rice
- 1/3 cup of seasoned breadcrumbs
- ¾ cup of reduced-sodium marinara sauce, divided
- ¼ cup of minced onion
- 1 oz. grated Parmesan cheese (about ¼ cup)
- 3 tbsp. of chopped parsley
- 2 tsp. of tomato paste
- ¼ tsp. of kosher salt
- Black pepper to taste
- 1 large egg, beaten
- 1 garlic clove, minced
- ½ cup of water
- 1 oz. of shredded mozzarella cheese (about ¼ cup)

Cooking Instructions:

1. In a medium bowl, combine together the chopped pepper tops with ground turkey, cooked brown rice and breadcrumbs.

2. Add ¼ cup of marinara sauce, onion, Parmesan cheese, parsley, tomato paste, salt, black pepper, egg, and garlic. Give everything a good mix.

3. Add 1 cup of ground turkey mixture into each pepper. Add ½ cup of water into the bottom of your Instant Pot and place the trivet.

4. Add the stand stuffed peppers upright on the trivet. Cover each pepper top with 2 tbsp. of marinara sauce. Secure the lid in place. Select Manual High Pressure for 15 minutes.

5. Do a natural pressure release and carefully open the lid. Top with mozzarella cheese, and cover until cheese melts, about 2 minutes.

6. Serve and enjoy!

Turkey Taco Pasta

Servings: 8 cups

Preparation time: 5 minutes

Cook time: 5 minutes

Total time: 10 minutes

Ingredients:

- 1 lb. of ground turkey
- ½ cup of sweet onion, chopped
- 2 tbsp. of taco seasoning
- 1 cup of frozen sweet corn
- 1 – 14.5 ounces can of fired roasted diced tomatoes
- 2 cups of chicken broth
- 8 oz. pasta of your choice, uncooked
- 1 ½ cups of sharp cheddar, shredded
- Garnishes: Freshly chopped cilantro, Freshly chopped green onion, Sour cream, Chopped red onion, Extra cheese, Fresh salsa and Shredded lettuce

Cooking Instructions:

1. Press the Sauté function on your Instant Pot and add the onion.

2. Add the ground turkey and cook while stirring until browned. When it has cooked through, add in the taco seasoning and frozen corn.

3. Add the fire roasted tomatoes, chicken broth and pasta. Secure the lid in place and ensure that the valve is in sealing position.

4. Select Manual High Pressure for 5 minutes. When the timer beeps, do a quick pressure release.

5. Carefully open the lid and stir the taco pasta together. Add the cheese to the pasta mixture.

6. Close the pot and allow the cheese to melt for about 2 minutes. Carefully open the lid and give everything a good stir.

7. Serve with your desired garnishes and enjoy!

Turkey & Pumpkin Chili

Preparation time: 15 minutes

Cook time: 30 minutes

Total time: 45 minutes

Serves: 4

Ingredients:

- 2 tbsp. of olive oil
- 1 medium brown onion, finely diced
- 1 celery stick, finely diced
- ½ tsp. of salt
- 1 long green chili pepper such as jalapeño, sliced (seeds left in)
- 3 cloves garlic, finely diced
- 1.5 pound / 700 g ground turkey or turkey steaks, diced
- 1 pound / 500-600 g kabocha squash or other sweet winter squash, peeled and diced into small cubes (about ½ of medium kabocha squash/Jap pumpkin)
- 2 cups of drained canned white beans/cannellini beans
- 2 cubes of chicken stock (we used organic Kallo brand)
- 2 tsp. of ground cumin
- 1 tsp. of dried coriander seed
- 1 can / 400 ml of full-fat coconut milk
- Juice of ½ lime
- To serve: fresh cilantro, scallions and chopped pickled jalapeños, extra lime, grated cheese (optional)

Cooking Instructions:

1. Press the Sauté setting on your Instant Pot and add the olive oil.

2. Add the onions, celery and salt. Cook for about 5 minutes, stirring a few times. Add the remaining ingredients, except for lime juice and garnishes.

3. Give everything a good stir. Secure the lid in place and ensure that the valve is in sealing position. Select the Poultry function to cook for 15 minutes.

4. When the timer beeps, do a natural pressure release for about 10 minutes, then quick release any remaining pressure.

5. Carefully remove the lid and add the lime juice. Season with more salt and add the chili. Press the Sauté function and cook for about 6 minutes with the lid off, stirring frequently.

6. Serve over cooked white or brown rice with freshly chopped cilantro, scallions, and pickled jalapeños.

7. Serve immediately and enjoy!

BEEF
Beef Ragu

Preparation time: 15 minutes

Cook time: 50 minutes

Total time: 1 hour 5 minutes

Serves: 4

Ingredients:

- 2 tbsp. of olive oil
- 1 medium brown onion, finely diced
- 1 large carrot, diced into small cubes
- 1 celery stick, diced into small cubes
- ½ long red chili, diced (or ½ tsp. chili flakes or cayenne pepper)
- 1 + ½ tsp. of sea salt
- 3 large cloves of garlic, finely diced
- 1.5 pound / 700-750 g diced beef steak (stewing steak, chuck steak, rib eye)
- 1 tsp. of black or white pepper
- 2 bay leaves
- 1 tsp. of ground paprika (mild or sweet)
- 1 tsp. of dried oregano, thyme or basil
- ½ tsp. of cinnamon powder (optional, but adds warmth and depth)
- 1 star anise (optional)
- 1 x can chopped tinned tomatoes (400 g/ 1 + ½ cups)
- 1 tbsp. of coconut Amino (or Tamari wheat-free soy sauce)
- 1 cube of beef stock including water

Cooking Instructions:

1. Press the Sauté function on your Instant Pot and add the olive oil.

2. Add the onions, carrots, celery, chili and salt and sauté for about 5 minutes, stirring occasionally, until softened.

3. Add the beef and the remaining ingredients and give everything a good stir. Secure the lid in place and ensure that the valve is in sealing position.

4. Select Manual, High pressure, and set for 30 minutes. When the timer beeps, do a natural pressure release for about 10 minutes, then quick release any remaining pressure.

5. Carefully remove the lid and use a potato masher to mash or shred the beef into smaller pieces.

6. Mash until your desired consistency is achieved. Cook for about 10 to 15 minutes to thicken the sauce, stirring every 2-3 minutes.

7. Serve with pasta, vegetable noodles or rice.

Beef Bourguignon

Preparation time: 20 minutes

Cook time: 55 minutes

Total time: 1 hour 15 minutes

Serves: 6

Ingredients:

- 2 medium brown onions, finely diced (or 7-8 small shallots, peeled)
- 4 slices of bacon or pancetta, diced
- 1 tbsp. of olive oil
- 3 cloves of crushed or finely diced garlic
- 3 pounds (1.5 kg) good quality braising beef steak, cut into cubes or diced beef
- 1+ ½ tsp. of sea salt
- ½ tsp. of ground black pepper
- 1 cup of stock (beef or chicken)
- 1 cup of red wine
- 1 cup of chopped tinned tomatoes
- 1 tsp. of mixed dried herbs
- 1 bay leaf
- 2 sprigs of rosemary
- 5 ounces (150 g) button mushrooms, sliced or left whole if they are small (Optional)
- 2 large carrots (sliced)

To Finish:

- 1 tbsp. of cornstarch, regular flour or tapioca flour
- 1 tbsp. of butter
- 2 tbsp. of freshly chopped parsley, to serve

Cooking Instructions:

1. Turn on your Instant Pot and press the Sauté function.

2. Add the olive oil, onion and bacon and sauté for about 5 minutes, stirring occasionally, until golden brown.

3. Add the garlic, beef, salt, pepper, stock, red wine, tomatoes, and herbs and give everything a good stir.

4. Add the mushrooms, if desired, and half of the carrots and set the other half aside.

5. Secure the lid in place and ensure that the valve is in sealing position. Select Manual, High pressure, and set for 30 minutes.

6. When the timer beeps, do a natural pressure release for about 10 minutes, then quick release any remaining pressure.

7. Carefully open the lid and add the remaining carrots. Set your Instant Pot to the Sauté function with the lid off.

8. Cook for about 10 minutes, stirring occasionally to thicken the sauce.

9. In a medium bowl, combine together the cornstarch or other flour with a few tablespoons or water or the broth from the stew.

10. Whisk together and add the mixture to the broth. Give everything a good stir and add the butter. Sprinkle with parsley over your desired vegetables or pasta.

11. Serve immediately and enjoy!

BBQ Beef Short Ribs

Preparation time: 10 minutes

Cook time: 40 minutes

Total time: 50 minutes

Serves: 2

Ingredients:

- 8 ounces (227 g) short ribs
- Sea salt and pepper
- 3 tsp. (15 ml) olive oil, avocado oil or lard
- 1 large onion, sliced into rings
- ½ cup (118 ml) high-quality store-bought ketchup
- ½ cup (118 ml) crushed tomatoes
- ¼ cup (60 ml) local honey
- ½ tsp. of onion powder
- 1 tsp. of (5 ml) liquid smoke
- ½ tsp. of garlic powder
- ½ tsp. of sea salt
- 1 tsp. (5 ml) gluten-free Worcestershire sauce (Optional)
- Fresh thyme, optional
- Potato salad & steamed greens, for serving

Cooking Instructions:

1. Generously season the short ribs with sea salt and pepper. Drizzle your stainless-steel bowl with cooking oil and press the Sauté function.

2. Add the seasoned ribs and onions into the oil. Sauté the ribs on each side for about 3 minutes.

3. In a medium bowl, combine together the ketchup, tomatoes, honey, onion powder, liquid smoke, garlic powder, sea salt and Worcestershire sauce and stir.

4. Add the sauce over the ribs. Secure the lid in place and ensure that the valve is in sealing position. Select Manual, High Pressure and set for 28 minutes.

5. When the timer beeps, do a quick pressure release. Carefully open the lid and remove the ribs from the sauce.

6. Ladle off the fat to reduce the BBQ sauce. Press the Sauté function again and let to simmer for about 10 minutes to thicken. Add the onions and sauce.

7. Spoon the sauce on top the ribs when your desired thickness is achieved. Garnish with fresh thyme if desired.

8. Serve with potato salad and steamed greens with bacon if desired.

Beef Chili

Preparation time: 10 minutes

Cook time: 10 minutes

Total time: 20 minutes

Ingredients:

- 1 pound of ground beef, venison, or turkey
- 2 onions, chopped
- 1 clove garlic, minced
- 1 green peppers
- 28 ounces diced tomatoes
- ½ pound of dry kidney beans (soaked overnight) OR 2 (14.5 ounces) cans
- 1 tablespoon of salt
- ½ tablespoon of chili powder
- Dash cayenne pepper

Cooking Instructions:

1. Spray your Instant Pot inner liner with a non-stick cooking spray.

2. Turn on the Meat setting on your Instant Pot and brown your meat. Add the onion and cook until translucent. Press Cancel to turn off the Meat function.

3. Add the rest of the ingredients. Secure the lid in place and ensure that the valve is in sealing position. Press the Soup function and set for 10 minutes.

4. When the timer beeps, do a quick pressure release. Carefully remove the lid and give everything a good stir.

5. Serve and enjoy!

Vietnamese Beef Brisket Tacos

Preparation time: 15 minutes

Cook time: 1 hour 25 minutes

Total time: 1 hour 40 minutes

Serves: 4

Ingredients:

- 1 tbsp. of sesame oil
- 1 small onion, sliced
- 4 garlic cloves, smashed
- 1 heaping tbsp. of minced, fresh ginger
- 1 (2- to 2½ lb.) brisket, at room temperature
- Salt and pepper
- ½ cup hoisin sauce
- 3 tbsp. of fish sauce
- 2 tbsp. of Sriracha or other hot sauce
- ¼ cup of water
- 2 cups of rainbow coleslaw mix
- 1 cucumber, cut into matchsticks
- 1 jalapeño, thinly sliced
- 2 tbsp. of chopped fresh cilantro
- 1 tbsp. of rice vinegar (regular vinegar)
- ½ lime, juiced
- Tortillas, warmed, for serving

Cooking Instructions:

1. Press the Sauté function on your Instant Pot and add the sesame oil.

2. Add the onion and sauté for 1 minute. Add the garlic and ginger, and cook for additional 2 minutes. Turn off the Sauté function.

3. Generously season the brisket with salt and pepper on each side and add into the bottom of your Instant Pot. Top with the hoisin sauce, fish sauce, sriracha, and water.

4. Secure the lid in place and ensure that the valve is in sealing position. Select Manual, High Pressure for 1 hour.

5. When the timer beeps, do a natural pressure release for about 10 minutes, then quick release any remaining pressure.

6. In a small bowl, combine together the coleslaw mix, cucumber, jalapeño, cilantro, rice vinegar, and lime juice. Add salt and pepper to taste and toss together.

7. Carefully open the lid and remove the brisket to a cutting board. Turn on the Sauté function and simmer the sauce for 10 minutes to thicken.

8. Turn off the Sauté function. Slice the brisket into thin pieces and discard any large pieces of fat. Add the brisket back into the pot and give everything a good stir.

9. Top warmed tortillas with sauce-coated brisket and slaw.

10. Serve and enjoy!

Italian Tomato Meatballs

Preparation time: 15 minutes

Cook time: 15 minutes

Total time: 30 minutes

Serves: 4

Ingredients:

For the Meatballs:

- 1.3 pound / 600 g ground beef (beef minced)
- 1 tsp. of onion powder
- 1 tsp. of garlic powder
- 1 tsp. of dried oregano
- 2 tsp. of ground paprika
- ½ tsp. of celery salt (optional, if not using, add ½ teaspoon of regular salt)
- 1 tsp. of salt

For the Sauce:

- 2 tbsp. of olive oil
- 1 brown onion, finely diced
- ½ long fresh red chili, chopped (or ½ teaspoon of red chili flakes or powder)
- 1 tsp. of salt
- 2 large garlic cloves, finely diced
- 1 can tinned diced chopped tomatoes (400 ml)

Cooking Instructions:

1. In a medium bowl, combine together the ground beef with the spices and salt.

2. Mix through with your hands and roll the mixture into small 2-inch balls and set aside. Press the Sauté function on your Instant Pot and add the olive oil.

3. Add the onions, chill and salt and cook for 5 minutes, stirring occasionally. Add the meatballs, sprinkle with garlic and pour over the tinned tomatoes. Give everything a good stir and spread the meatballs evenly in the sauce.

4. Secure the lid in place and ensure that the valve is in sealing position. When the timer beeps, do a natural pressure release for about 10 minutes, then quick release any remaining pressure.

5. Carefully open the lid and give everything a good stir. Serve over spaghetti, rice, sliced baguettes or with a side of cauliflower rice or steamed vegetables.

Chunky Beef, Cabbage & Tomato Soup

Preparation time: 10 minutes

Cook time: 20 minutes

Total time: 30 minutes

Ingredients:

- 1 pound 90% lean ground beef
- 1 - ½ tsp. of kosher salt
- ½ cup of diced onion
- ½ cup of diced celery
- ½ cup of diced carrot
- 28 ounces can diced or crushed tomatoes
- 5 cups of chopped green cabbage
- 4 cups of beef stock (canned or homemade)
- 2 bay leaves

Cooking Instructions:

1. Press the Sauté function on your Instant Pot and add the olive oil.

2. Add the ground beef and salt and sauté until browned, breaking up meat into small pieces for about 4 minutes.

3. When browned, add the onion, celery and carrots and cook for 5 minutes. Add the tomatoes, cabbage, beef stock and bay leaves.

4. Secure the lid in place and ensure that the valve is in sealing position. Select Manual, High Pressure for 20 minutes.

5. When the timer beeps, do a natural pressure release for about 10 minutes, then quick release any remaining pressure.

6. Carefully open the lid and discard the bay leaves.

7. Serve immediately and enjoy!

Beef Picadillo

Preparation time: 10 minutes

Cook time: 15 minutes

Total time: 25 minutes

Ingredients:

- 1 - ½ pound 93% lean ground beef
- ½ medium onion, chopped
- 2 cloves garlic, minced
- 1 tomato, chopped
- 1 tsp. of kosher salt
- ½ red bell pepper, finely chopped
- 2 tablespoons of cilantro
- 4 ounces (1/2 can) tomato sauce
- 1 teaspoon of ground cumin
- 1-2 bay leaf
- 2 tablespoons alcaparrado (capers or green olives)

Cooking Instructions:

1. Press the Sauté function on your Instant Pot and add the meat.

2. Brown the meat and season with salt and pepper. Break up the meat into smaller pieces with a wooden spoon and cook until no longer pink.

3. Add the onion, garlic, tomato, salt, pepper and cilantro and stir for 1 minute. Add the alcaparrado or olives and about 2 tablespoons of brine or juice from the olives.

4. Add the cumin, and bay leaf. Add tomato sauce and 3 tablespoons of water and give everything a good mix.

5. Secure the lid in place and ensure that the valve is in sealing position. Select Manual, High Pressure for 15 minutes.

6. When the timer beeps, do a natural pressure release and carefully open the lid. Give everything a good stir.

7. Serve and enjoy!

Beef & Chorizo Chili

Preparation time: 15 minutes

Cook time: 20 minutes

Total time: 35 minutes

Serves: 5-6

Ingredients:

- 1½ tbsp. of olive oil or coconut oil
- 1 large brown onion, chopped
- 1 medium carrot (or 2 small ones), peeled and diced into small cubes
- 1 celery stick, diced into small cubes
- 7 ounces / 200 g chorizo sausage, peeled and diced
- 1 long red chili, finely diced
- 2.2 pound / 1 kg ground beef (grass-fed, if possible)
- 3 cloves garlic, finely diced
- 2 tsp. of ground cumin
- 2 tsp. of ground coriander seed
- 2 cups / about 400 g tinned chopped tomatoes
- 4 tbsp. of tomato paste
- 1 tbsp. of Tamari or soy sauce (coconut aminos)
- 2 tsp. of salt
- 2 bay leaves
- 3 tbsp. of port or fortified red wine (optional)
- To serve: flash pan-fried zucchini or cooked white rice, chopped avocado and cilantro.

Cooking Instructions:

1. Press the Sauté setting on your Instant Pot and add the oil.

2. Add the onion, carrot, celery, chorizo and chili and sauté for about 3 to 4 minutes. Add the beef, garlic, spices and stir. Add the tinned tomatoes and paste.

3. Add the remaining ingredients and give everything a good stir. Press Keep Warm/Cancel function. Secure the lid in place and ensure that the valve is in sealing position. Select Manual, High Pressure for 15 minutes.

4. When the timer beeps, do a natural pressure release for about 10 minutes, then quick release any remaining pressure. Carefully remove the lid and stir.

5. Serve and enjoy!

Korean Ground Beef Bulgogi

Preparation time: 10 minutes

Cook time: 10 minutes

Total time: 20 minutes

Ingredients:

- 2 tbsp. of oil
- 6 cloves garlic, minced
- 2-inch knob ginger, minced
- 2 lb. of ground beef
- ½ cup of coconut sugar
- ⅔ cup of coconut amino
- 1 tsp. of crushed red pepper flakes
- 1 tsp. of salt
- ½ tsp. of black pepper
- 6 green onions, thinly sliced
- 2 tbsp. of sesame oil
- 2 tsp. of sesame seeds

Cooking Instructions:

1. Press the Sauté function on your Instant Pot and add the oil.

2. Add the garlic and ginger and sauté for 2 to 3 minutes. Add the ground beef to the pot and cook until brown. Add the rest of the ingredients and mix well.

3. Secure the lid in place and ensure that the valve is in sealing position. Select Manual, High Pressure for 10 minutes.

4. When the timer beeps, do a natural pressure release for about 10 minutes, then quick release any remaining pressure.

5. Carefully remove the lid and stir the green onions, sesame oil and sesame seeds into the pot. Give everything a good stir

6. Serve and enjoy!

PORK

Savory Pork Burrito Bowls

Preparation time: 10 minutes

Cook time: 45 minutes

Total time: 55 minutes

Servings: 6

Ingredients:

For the Meat:

- 2 ½ pounds of pork country style ribs
- 1 cup of salsa or picante sauce
- 1 teaspoon of garlic powder
- 1 teaspoon of chili powder
- 1 teaspoon of cumin
- 1 cup of water
- 1 tablespoon of lime juice, (Optional)

For the Burrito Bowls:

- Burrito bowl items: cilantro, lime wedges, romaine lettuce, tomatoes, pico de gallo, shredded cheese, black beans, brown rice, guacamole, sour cream, etc.

Cooking Instructions:

1. Add the pork into the bottom of your Instant Pot and add the salsa.

2. Add the garlic powder, chili powder, cumin and water. Secure the lid in place and ensure that the valve is in sealing position.

3. Select Manual, High Pressure for 45 minutes for frozen pork country style, 30 minutes for thawed pork country style ribs, 30 minutes for frozen boneless and 30 minutes for thawed beef chuck roast.

4. When the timer beeps, do a natural pressure release for about 10 minutes, then quick release any remaining pressure.

5. Carefully open the lid and shred the meat. Stir in the lime juice, if desired and give everything a good stir.

6. Serve meat with desired burrito bowl items and enjoy!

Smoked Pulled Pork

Preparation time: 30 minutes

Cook time: 70 minutes

Total time: 90 minutes

Servings: 12

Ingredients:

- 3 ½ pounds of pork carnitas meat, shoulder or butt roast
- 1 cup of chicken broth
- 2 tablespoons of soy sauce (We used low sodium soy sauce)
- 2 tablespoons of liquid smoke
- 2 garlic cloves, minced

Cooking Instructions:

1. Quarter the pork and add them into the bottom of your Instant Pot.

2. Add all the remaining ingredients over the top of the pork. Secure the lid in place and close the vent.

3. Select Manual, High Pressure for 70 minutes. When the timer beeps, do a natural pressure release for about 15 minutes.

4. Carefully open the lid and place the meat to a cutting board. Shred the meat with two forks. Add the meat back into your pot and give everything a good stir.

5. Serve and enjoy!

Pork Vindaloo

Servings: 6

Preparation time: 10 minutes

Cook time: 25 minutes

Total time: 35 minutes

Ingredients:

- 3 lbs. (1.44 kg) boneless pork shoulder, cubed
- 1 tsp. of sea salt
- ¼ cup (60 ml) olive oil
- 1 large white onion, peeled and finely chopped
- 4 cloves garlic, peeled and minced
- 1 piece fresh ginger, peeled and grated
- 2 tbsp. of vindaloo seasoning or Madras curry
- 1 tsp. of hot paprika
- ½ tsp. of ground turmeric
- 3 tbsp. of all-purpose flour
- 1/3 cup (80 ml) Champagne vinegar
- 1 (14 ½ ounce) can diced tomatoes in juice, undrained
- 1 cup (250 ml) reduced-sodium chicken broth

Cooking Instructions:

1. Sprinkle the cubed pork with a slat. Press the Sauté function on your Instant Pot and add 2 tbsp. of oil.

2. Working in batches, brown the pork in a single layer on all sides for about 6 minutes per batch. Place the browned pork to a bowl with a slotted spoon.

3. Add the chopped white onion and sauté, stirring until soft for about 3 minutes. Stir in garlic, ginger, and spices.

4. Cook, stirring for additional 30 seconds. Sprinkle in all-purpose flour and give everything a good stir. Add the browned pork to your Instant Pot.

5. Stir in vinegar, tomatoes with their juice and chicken broth. Deglaze the pot by scrapping with a slotted spoon to remove any brown bits stuck to the bottom of your pot.

6. Bring to a boil over medium-high heat. Secure the lid in place and ensure that the valve is in sealing position. Select Manual, High Pressure for 25 minutes.

7. When the timer beeps, do a natural pressure release for about 10 minutes, then quick release any remaining pressure.

8. Carefully open the lid and skim any fat from the top of the sauce. Let to sit for about 15 minutes.

9. Sprinkle with fresh chopped cilantro and serve immediately.

Mexican Pulled Pork

Preparation time: 20 minutes

Cook time: 1 hour 10 minutes

Total time: 1 hour 30 minutes

Servings: 16-20

Ingredients:

- 1 large onion, cut into large slices
- 2 cups of chicken broth (or water with chicken bouillon)
- 4-5 pounds of pork carnitas meat or pork shoulder, trimmed of excess fat
- 1 (15 ounces) can diced tomato with jalapenos
- 2 tablespoons tomato paste
- 1 ½ teaspoon of garlic salt
- ¼ teaspoon of pepper
- 1 teaspoon of oregano

Cooking Instructions:

1. Add the onions into the bottom of your Instant Pot.

2. Add the broth and pork on top of the onions. Secure the lid in place and close the vent. Select Manual, High Pressure for 70 minutes.

3. When the timer beeps, do a natural pressure release for about 20 minutes. Carefully open the lid and place the meat on a cutting board.

4. Discard the onions and any liquid in the pot. Shred the meat with two forks and add them back to the pot. Add in tomatoes, tomato paste, garlic salt, pepper and oregano.

5. Give everything a good stir until meat is coated. Season with extra salt and pepper to taste. Add a can of tomato sauce to make it saucy if desired.

6. Serve meat in tacos, burritos, enchiladas, salads, sandwiches etc.

Pork Barbecue Sandwiches

Preparation time: 10 minutes

Cook time: 1 hour

Total time: 1 hour 10 minutes

Ingredients:

- 2.5 – 3 pounds of boneless pork roast or shoulder, trimmed of fat
- 3 tablespoons of brown sugar
- 2 tablespoons of chili powder
- 2 tablespoons of paprika
- 1 teaspoon of cumin
- 1 teaspoon of sea salt
- ½ teaspoon of black pepper
- ¾ cup of apple cider
- ½ cup of Barbecue sauce
- ¼ cup of Buffalo wing hot sauce
- 8 hamburger buns or sandwich rolls

Cooking Instructions:

1. Cut the pork against the grain in half and reserve aside.

2. In a medium bowl, combine together the brown sugar, chili powder, paprika, cumin, salt, and pepper.

3. Season the pork roast with the seasonings on all sides. Add the barbecue sauce, apple cider, and buffalo sauce into the bottom of your Instant Pot and give everything a good stir. Add the pork on top.

4. Secure the lid in place and close the vent. Select Manual, High Pressure for 45 minutes. When the timer beeps, do a natural pressure release.

5. Carefully open the lid and place the pork to a cutting board. Shred the pork with two forks, discard any excess fat.

6. Add the pork back into the pot with the sauce and give everything a good mix.

7. Serve on top of hamburger buns or sandwiches with your desired toppings.

Creamy Mushroom Sauce Pork

Preparation time: 2 minutes

Cook time: 20 minutes

Total time: 22 minutes

Servings: 4

Ingredients:

- 2 pounds of pork (country style ribs, pork chops, pork loin, pork shoulder)
- 1 (13.75 ounces) can cream of mushroom soup
- ¾ cup of water (or chicken broth)
- Salt and pepper
- Cornstarch, (Optional)

Cooking Instructions:

1. Add the ¾ cup of water (or chicken broth) into the bottom of your Instant Pot.

2. Add the pork and season with salt and pepper. Place cream of mushroom soup on top of the pork.

3. Secure the lid in place and close the vent. Select Manual, High Pressure for 20 minutes. When the timer beeps, do a natural pressure release for about 15 minutes.

4. Carefully open the lid. Add 1 to 2 tbsp. of cornstarch and mix with 1 to 2 tbsp. of cold to thicken the sauce and stirring until smooth if desired.

5. Stir the slurry into the Instant Pot and sauté on High mode high until the sauce has thickened.

6. Shred the pork and serve with the sauce.

Salsa Pork Chops

Servings: 6

Preparation time: 5 minutes

Cook time: 15 minutes

Total time: 20 minutes

Ingredients:

- 6 bone-in center cut pork chops, about 1/2 inch thick
- Kosher salt and black pepper to taste
- 3 tbsp. of olive oil
- 1 - 24 ounces jar chunky salsa (We used a zesty cilantro version)

Cooking Instructions:

1. Generously season the pork chops with salt and pepper on both sides.

2. Press the Sauté function on your Instant Pot and add the olive oil. When hot, sauté the pork chops 1 or 2 at a time.

3. Cook each pork chop for about 1-2 minutes per side working in batches until browned.

4. Add half of the pork chops back into the bottom of your Instant Pot and top with half jar of salsa. Add rest of the pork chops and top with remaining salsa.

5. Secure the lid in place and close the vent. Select Manual, High Pressure for 2 minutes.

6. When the timer beeps, do a natural pressure release for about 10 minutes. Check for doneness with a meat thermometer. The pork chop should read about 145°F.

7. Carefully open the lid and place the pork chops on a cutting board. Drain the salsa with a slotted spoon.

8. Shred the pork with two forks and add them back into the pot. Give everything a good stir.

9. Serve immediately and enjoy!

Mississippi Pork Sandwiches

Preparation time: 15 minutes

Cook time: 80 minutes

Total time: 95 minutes

Servings: 8

Ingredients:

- 2 lbs. of pork loin roast
- ¼ cup of butter, divided
- ½ cup of water
- 1 tablespoon of Better than Bouillon Chicken Base
- ½ cup of pepperoncini juice
- 5 pepperoncini's
- 1 teaspoon of kosher salt
- 1 teaspoon of onion powder
- 1 teaspoon of garlic powder
- ¼ teaspoon of dried thyme
- ¼ teaspoon of black pepper
- Buns
- Provolone cheese

Cooking Instructions:

1. Press the Sauté function on your Instant Pot. When hot, add 2 tablespoons of butter.

2. Cut your pork roast in half in and add in the roast pieces into your pot. Allow each piece to brown for about 5 minutes per side.

3. When it has browned, remove the roast and add in a bowl. Deglaze the pot with water to scrape any browned bit stuck to the bottom of your pot.

4. Add in the Better than Bouillon and dissolve it in the water. Add pepperoncini juice and roast back into the pot. Nestle the pepperoncini's around the roast.

5. Add another 2 tablespoons of butter. Sprinkle the roast with the salt, onion powder, garlic powder, thyme and black pepper.

6. Secure the lid in place and close the vent. Select Manual, High Pressure for 80 minutes. When the timer beeps, do a natural pressure release for about 15 minutes.

7. Carefully open the lid and remove the roast and add on a cutting board. Shred the roast and add them back into your pot. Stir it in with the juices.

8. Serve shredded meat on toasted buns with melted provolone cheese on top.

Crispy Pork Carnitas

Preparation time: 20 minutes

Cook time: 70 minutes

Total time: 90 minutes

Servings: 4-6

Ingredients:

- 1 red onion, quartered
- 1 cup of chicken broth
- 2 bay leaves
- 2 ½ - 3 pounds of pork (We used "carnitas meat" from Winco)
- 3 garlic cloves, peeled
- 1 jalapeno, diced
- 1 teaspoon of kosher salt
- ½ teaspoon of black pepper
- 2 teaspoons of dried oregano
- 2 teaspoons of cumin
- ¼ cup of lime juice
- Salt and pepper to taste

Cooking Instructions:

1. Add the quartered onion into the bottom of your Instant Pot.

2. Add the chicken broth, bay leaves, pork, garlic and jalapeno. Sprinkle the pork with the salt, pepper, oregano and cumin. Secure the lid in place and close the vent.

3. Select Manual, High Pressure for 70 minutes. When the timer beeps, do a natural pressure release for about 15 minutes. Carefully open the lid and shred the meat on a cutting board.

4. Reserve the juices and turn your oven to broil. Add the meat in a foil-lined pan and spread out the meat. Add the pan in your oven to broil for about 5 minutes.

5. Add about ¼ cup of the juices from your Instant Pot over the meat. Place in your oven for additional 5 minutes, or until your desired crispiness is achieved. Salt and pepper the meat.

6. Toss the meat with the lime juice and any extra juices. Serve with your desired toppings like salads, burritos, tacos, enchiladas, quesadillas etc.

VEGAN & VEGETARIAN
Broccoli Soup with Gremolata

Preparation time: 15 minutes

Cook time: 15 minutes

Total time: 30 minutes

Serves: 4

Ingredients:

- 2 tbsp. of olive oil
- 1 medium brown onion, peeled and finely diced
- 1 large celery stick, diced
- 1 pound / 450-500 g broccoli, cut into quarters and the stems diced roughly
- 2 medium white potatoes (350 g / 0.7 pound), peeled and diced into small cubes
- 2 large cloves of garlic, diced
- 1 liter of water or/and vegetable stock (4 x 250 ml cups)
- 2 + ½ tsp. of salt (use less if using vegetable stock)
- ½ tsp. of pepper
- ½ cup of coconut cream/milk (Optional)

For Gremolata:

- 1 lemon, zest only
- Large handful of fresh parsley, finely chopped
- 1 small garlic clove, finely chopped (optional)

Cooking Instructions:

1. Turn on the Instant Pot and set to Sauté function. Add the olive oil, onions and celery. Sauté for about 3-4 minutes, stirring a few times.

2. Add the remaining ingredients (except for the lemon and parsley) and stir through. Press Cancel/Keep Warm to stop the sauté function.

3. Secure the lid in place and close the vent. Select Manual, High Pressure for 3 minutes.

4. When the timer beeps, do a natural pressure release for about 10 minutes, then quick release any remaining pressure.

5. Grate the peel of the lemon and chop the parsley. A peeler can also be used to cut off the rind and chop it very finely.

6. In a medium bowl, combine together the lemon zest and parsley if desired and set aside. Add the juice of ½ lemon to the soup mixture.

7. Transfer the soup, in batches, to a food processor or a blender and puree the soup. Add them back to your pot.

8. Stir in the coconut cream or crème fraiche/sour cream. Season with more salt and pepper, if you desired.

9. Serve, topped with a teaspoon or two of the gremolata.

Vegetables En Papillote

Preparation time: 10 minutes

Cook time: 10 minutes

Total time: 20 minutes

Serves: 2-3

Ingredients:

- 2-3 ounces of fine green beans, tails chopped off
- 4 small carrots, peeled and sliced into long sticks
- ¼ tsp. of cracked black pepper
- ½ tsp. of sea salt
- 1 large garlic clove, sliced
- 1 tbsp. of butter or olive oil
- 1 tbsp. of lemon juice
- 1 slice of lemon
- 1 tbsp. of fresh herbs (We used fresh oregano leaves but you can add rosemary, thyme, parsley)
- 15" (30-35cm square) of parchment/baking paper

Cooking Instructions:

1. Add the wire rack into the bottom of your Instant Pot and pour 1 cup of water.

2. Place a piece of parchment paper on a cutting board and add the vegetables in the middle. Generously season with pepper and salt, scatter the garlic around.

3. Top with a few dollops of butter and drizzle with lemon juice. Add the lemon slice in the middle and sprinkle with fresh herbs.

4. Gently fold the paper in half to form a parcel, fold the edges together tightly. Place the parcel onto the wire rack inside the pot.

5. Secure the lid in place and close the vent. Select Manual, High Pressure for 2 minutes. When the timer beeps, do a natural pressure release for about 2 minutes, then quick release any remaining pressure.

6. Carefully remove the lid and transfer the parcel out of the pot and onto a plate. Open the parcel at the table.

7. Serve and enjoy!

Tangy Egg & Cheese Salad

Preparation time: 15 minutes

Cook time: 10 minutes

Total time: 25 minutes

Serves: 8

Ingredients:

- 8 large free-range chicken eggs
- 1 + ½ cup grated hard cheese, such as Cheddar or Mozzarella
- 2 large cloves of garlic, finely diced or grated
- ⅓ Cup of mayonnaise (about 5-6 tbsp.)
- 1 tsp. of Dijon or yellow mustard (optional)
- Pinch of salt and pepper

Cooking Instructions:

1. Add a trivet on the bottom of your Instant Pot and pour a cup of water.

2. Add the eggs on top of the trivet. Secure the lid in place and close the vent. Select Manual, High Pressure for 5 minutes.

3. When the timer beeps, do a natural pressure release for about 5 minutes, then quick release any remaining pressure.

4. Carefully open the lid and transfer the eggs and place in a bowl with cold water for a couple of minutes. To make the salad, peel the eggs and grate or finely dice into a mixing bowl.

5. Set one egg yolk aside garnishing later. Add the remaining ingredients and give everything a good mix.

6. Garnish with crumbled egg yolk, black pepper and some fresh parsley on top.

7. Serve with veggies sticks or slices, with lettuce cups or your desired crackers.

Mexican Bean Salad

Preparation time: 15 minutes

Cook time: 30 minutes

Total time: 45 minutes

Serves: 4

Ingredients:

- ½ cup of dried white beans, soaked in water for 2-3 hours
- ½ cup of dried black beans, soaked in water for 2-3 hours
- 3 cups of water
- 1 tsp. of salt
- 1 cup of diced red bell pepper
- 8-10 cherry tomatoes, halved (or 2 medium tomatoes, diced)
- ⅓ cup of chopped scallions / green onions
- ¼ cup of chopped cilantro / coriander
- ½ long red chili, chopped
- 3 tbsp. of lime juice
- 3 tbsp. of olive oil
- ½ tsp. of coriander seed powder
- 1 garlic clove, grated or minced
- ¼ tsp. of salt (or to taste)
- Other options: diced avocado, tortilla chips, chopped jalapenos

Cooking Instructions:

1. Strain and rinse the pre-soaked beans. Place the beans into the bottom of your Instant Pot together with 3 cups of water and 1 tsp. salt.

2. Give everything a good stir. Secure the lid in place and close the vent. Select Manual, High Pressure for 12 minutes.

3. When the timer beeps, do a natural pressure release for about 15 minutes, then quick release any remaining pressure.

4. Strain and rinse the cooked beans, leave in the sieve to cool down. Add the cooked beans to a mixing bowl together with the remaining salad ingredients and give everything a good mix.

5. Serve and enjoy!

Easy Curried Coconut Lentils

Preparation time: 15 minutes

Cook time: 20 minutes

Total time: 35 minutes

Serves: 4-6

Ingredients:

- 2 cups of dried lentils (250 ml cups)
- 2 tbsp. of coconut oil or olive oil
- 1 medium brown onion, finely diced
- 1 large celery stick, finely diced
- 1 large carrot, finely diced
- 1 tsp. of salt
- 2 heaped tsp. of mild curry powder
- 2 cloves of garlic, finely diced
- 4-5 cherry tomatoes, halved (or 1 medium tomato, chopped)
- 1 can coconut milk (mix well before opening), about 400 ml
- 1 + ¼ cups of vegetable stock (or water + 1 vegetable stock cube)
- Juice of ½ lime
- Garnish with fresh cilantro/coriander

Cooking Instructions:

1. Rinse and drain the lentils and reserve aside. Turn on your Instant Pot and select the Sauté function.

2. When hot, add the oil and slightly heat up, then add the onions, carrots, celery and salt and sauté for about 5 minutes. Add the curry powder, lentils, garlic and tomatoes.

3. Give everything a good stir. Add the coconut milk and vegetable stock and stir through. Cancel the Sauté function. Secure the lid in place and close the vent.

4. Select Manual, High Pressure for 5 minutes. When the timer beeps, do a natural pressure release for about 10 minutes, then quick release any remaining pressure.

5. Carefully remove the lid and add the lime juice and stir the lentils. Give everything a good stir.

6. Serve with fresh cilantro/coriander on top.

Vegan Lentil Chili

Preparation time: 10 minutes

Cook time: 19 minutes

Total time: 44 minutes

Servings: 6

Ingredients:

- 1 tbsp. of olive oil
- 1 onion, chopped
- 4 cloves minced garlic
- 2 carrots, chopped
- 1-2 jalapeños, chopped
- 1 ½ tbsp. of chili powder
- 1 tbsp. of cumin
- ½ tsp. of ground coriander
- 1 tsp. of dried oregano
- ½ - ¾ tsp. of salt
- 1 (15 oz.) can crushed tomatoes
- 1 (28 oz.) can fire roasted diced tomatoes
- 2 cups of brown or green lentils (We used French green lentils)
- 4 cups of vegetable broth
- 1 tsp. of fresh lime juice
- ½ cup of chopped fresh cilantro

Cooking Instructions:

1. Turn on the Instant Pot and set to Sauté function.

2. When hot, add the oil, then the onion, garlic, carrots and jalapeños and cook until soft, for about 3-4 minutes.

3. Add the spices and rest of the ingredients except for lime juice and cilantro. Secure the lid in place and close the vent. Select Manual, High Pressure for 15 minutes.

4. When the timer beeps, do a quick pressure release. Carefully open the lid and stir in lime juice and cilantro. Give everything a good stir.

5. Serve and enjoy!

Walnut Lentil Tacos

Preparation time: 10 minutes

Cook time: 15 minutes

Total time: 25 minutes

Yield: 11-12 tacos

Ingredients:

- 1 white onion, diced
- 1 tbsp. of olive oil
- 1 garlic clove, minced
- 1 tbsp. of chili powder
- ½ tsp. of garlic powder
- ¼ tsp. of onion powder
- ¼ tsp. of red pepper flakes
- ¼ tsp. of oregano
- ½ tsp. of paprika
- 1 ½ tsp. of ground cumin
- ½ tsp. of kosher salt
- ¼ tsp. of freshly ground pepper
- 2 ¼ cups of vegetable broth
- 1 15 oz. can fire-roasted diced tomatoes
- ¾ cup of chopped walnuts
- 1 cup of dried brown lentils
- Taco toppings of choice: shredded lettuce, tomato, jalapenos
- Flour or corn tortillas

Cooking Instructions:

1. Press the Sauté function and add the olive oil when hot.

2. Add the onion and garlic clove and cook until onion is tender, stirring for about 3-4 minutes. Add the spices and stir.

3. Add the vegetable broth, tomatoes, walnuts and lentils and give everything a good stir to combine. Secure the lid in place and close the vent.

4. Select Manual, High Pressure for 15 minutes. When the timer beeps, do a quick pressure release. Carefully open the lid and stir lentils, seasoning to taste if desired.

5. Serve lentils on tortillas of choice with toppings.

Vegan Potato Curry

Preparation time: 10 minutes

Cook time: 40 minutes

Total time: 50 minutes

Servings: 5

Calories: 258 kcal

Ingredients:

- 1 medium yellow onion, chopped
- 4 large cloves of garlic, chopped finely
- 900g / about 5 heaping cups baby potatoes, or regular potatoes and cut any larger ones into chunky bite sized pieces.
- 2 tbsp. of curry powder or curry paste
- 500mls / around 2 cups water
- 400g / 2 heaping cups of fresh green beans, chopped into bite sized pieces.
- 1 400ml can coconut milk, full fat or light
- 1 tbsp. of sugar (optional)
- Salt & pepper to taste
- 1 tsp. of chili pepper flakes or a small fresh chili chopped (optional)
- 3 tbsp. of arrowroot powder, or corn starch

Cooking Instructions:

1. Set your Instant Pot to Sauté function and add a few drops of water. Add the onion and cook until translucent. Add the garlic and sauté for 1 minute.

2. Press the Cancel/Keep Warm function to stop sauté process. Add all the remaining ingredients except the green beans and arrowroot/cornstarch. Secure the lid in place and close the vent.

3. Select Manual, High Pressure for 20 minutes. When the timer beeps, do a natural pressure release for about 15 minutes. Carefully open the lid and press the Sauté function.

4. In a medium bowl, add the arrowroot/cornstarch and mix into it a few tablespoons of water. Pour the mixture into the pot stirring to make it thicker.

5. Season with salt and pepper to taste, add the green beans and cook for about 5 minutes until they are tender and the gravy has thickened.

6. Serve immediately and enjoy!

Quinoa Enchiladas

Preparation time: 5 minutes

Cook time: 1 minute

Total time: 6 minutes

Ingredients:

Homemade Enchilada Sauce:

- 3 tbsp. of oil (We used canola)
- 3 tbsp. of all-purpose flour
- 1 tbsp. of chili powder
- 1 ½ tsp. of cumin
- ½ tsp. of oregano
- ½ tsp. of garlic powder
- ¼ tsp. of salt
- 1/8 tsp. of cinnamon
- ¼ tsp. of cayenne pepper
- 1 (15 oz.) can crushed tomatoes
- 1 cup of water (or vegetable broth)

Enchilada Ingredients:

- 2 bell peppers, chopped
- 1 medium onion, chopped
- 1 cup enchilada sauce
- 1 medium zucchini, chopped
- 1 cup of uncooked quinoa
- ¾ cup of water
- 1 (15 oz.) can black beans, drained and rinsed
- 1 (15 oz.) can corn, drained and rinsed
- 1 (4 oz.) can diced jalapeños
- ¼ cup of fresh cilantro
- 4 corn tortillas, cut into strips
- 1 cup shredded cheddar cheese

Cooking Instructions:

1. Heat up the oil in a medium saucepan over medium heat to make the enchilada sauce.

2. Stir in the flour and cook for about 4 minutes or until golden brown, stirring often. Add the remaining spices: chili powder, cumin, garlic powder, oregano, salt, cinnamon, cayenne and stir for additional 1 minute until toasted.

3. Whisk in the crushed tomatoes and water and stir until thickened for about 6 minutes. Drain 1 cup of the sauce and reserve the remaining aside for drizzling.

4. Turn on the Instant Pot on and press the Sauté function. Add the bell peppers, onion, zucchini and a drizzle of olive oil and pinch of salt.

5. Cook, stirring occasionally until the vegetables are soft. Add in the uncooked quinoa and cook for additional 1 or 2 minutes until just toasted.

6. Hit the Cancel function on your Instant Pot and pour in the water and 1 cup of the enchilada sauce. Secure the lid in place and close the vent.

7. Select Manual, High Pressure for 1 minute. When the timer beeps, do a natural pressure release for about 15 minutes.

8. Carefully open the lid and stir in the black beans, corn, jalapeno, cheese, and cilantro and corn tortillas.

9. Serve warm, with extra enchilada sauce if desired.

APPETIZERS
Sweet and Spicy Meatballs

Preparation time: 5 minutes

Cook time: 25 minutes

Total time: 30 minutes

Ingredients:

- 16 ounces Cooked Perfect Meatballs
- 12 oz. of chili sauce
- 12 oz. of grape jelly
- ½ cup of water
- ½ tbsp. of crushed red pepper
- ½ tsp. of cayenne pepper
- Garnish: chopped green onions (optional)

Cooking Instructions:

1. Add the 16 ounces of Cooked Perfect Meatballs into the bottom of your Instant Pot.

2. In a small bowl, combine together the chili sauce, grape jelly, water and spices. Give everything a good stir to combine.

3. Add the mixture over Cooked Perfect Meatballs and stir to cover. Secure the lid in place and close the vent.

4. Select Manual, High Pressure for 10 minutes. Add your lid to the Instant Pot and set to Manual for 10 minutes.

5. When the timer beeps, do a natural pressure release for about 10 minutes, then quick release any remaining pressure.

6. Carefully open the lid and allow the meatballs sit to thicken the sauce.

7. Garnish with chopped green onions if desired and serve immediately.

Brisket Sliders with Caramelized Onions

Preparation time: 10 minutes

Cook time: 50 minutes

Total time: 1 hour

Servings: 6

Calories: 601 kcal

Ingredients:

- 1 ½ pounds of brisket
- 1-2 tablespoons of Stubbs's Beef Spice Rub
- 2 tablespoons of olive oil
- 1 tablespoon of liquid smoke
- 12 slider buns
- 2 cups of beef broth
- 2 onions, caramelized
- 6 slices of Provolone cheese
- ¼ cup of Stubbs's Sticky Sweet Bar-B-Q Sauce
- ¼ cup of butter, melted
- ½ teaspoon of onion powder
- ½ teaspoon of garlic powder

Cooking Instructions:

1. Remove brisket from fridge. Pat dry with a paper towel and season with Stubbs's Beef Spice Rub.

2. Add them back to the fridge for about 30 minutes. Remove from fridge. Press the Sauté function on your Instant Pot and add the olive oil.

3. Sauté the Brisket to brown on all sides. Add liquid smoke and beef broth. Secure the lid in place and close the vent.

4. Select Manual, High Pressure for 50 minutes. When the timer beeps, do a natural pressure release.

5. Carefully open the lid and remove the brisket and shred with two forks. Preheat your oven to 350 degrees.

6. Place the bottom of the sliders buns in your 2 quart baking dish. Top with shredded brisket, Stubbs's Sticky Sweet Bar-B-Q Sauce, caramelized onions, cheese and the top of the bun.

7. In a medium bowl, mix together the butter, onion powder and garlic powder. Brush over slider buns with the mixture.

8. Bake from 10-15 minutes or until cheese is melted and buns are golden brown on top.

9. Serve and enjoy!

Buffalo Chicken Dip

Preparation time: 10 minutes

Cook time: 7 minutes

Total time: 17 minutes

Serves: 12-15

Ingredients:

- 2 chicken breasts, skinless and boneless
- ½ cup of buffalo chicken sauce
- ¼ cup water
- 4 ounces of cream cheese (half a container)
- 4 ounces of ranch or blue cheese dressing, optional
- 1 stalk celery, chopped, optional
- ½ - 1 cup shredded cheese, optional
- Salt and pepper, to taste

Cooking Instructions:

1. Add the buffalo chicken sauce, water and chicken into the bottom of your Instant Pot.

2. Secure the lid in place and close the vent. Select Manual, High Pressure for 7 minutes.

3. When the timer beeps, do a natural pressure release for about 10 minutes, then quick release any remaining pressure.

4. Carefully open the lid and shred the chicken using two forks. Stir in the cheese and dressing, if desired.

5. Scoop the buffalo dip into your serving bowl and serve with chips or veggies for dipping.

6. Serve and enjoy!

Cilantro Lime Chicken Drumsticks

Preparation time: 11 minutes

Cook time: 9 minutes

Total time: 20 minutes

Ingredients:

- 1 tablespoon of olive oil
- 6 drumsticks
- 4 cloves minced garlic
- 1 teaspoon of crushed red peppers
- 1 teaspoon of cayenne pepper
- 1 teaspoon of salt
- Juice from 1 lime
- 2 tablespoons of chopped cilantro
- ½ cup of chicken broth

Cooking Instructions:

1. Turn on the Instant Pot and set to Sauté function.

2. Add the olive oil. Add the drumsticks and sprinkle the seasoning over the drumsticks. Stir the drumsticks with tongs and brown on each side for 2 minutes.

3. Add the lime juice, cilantro, and chicken broth to the Instant Pot. Secure the lid in place and close the vent.

4. Select Manual, High Pressure for 9 minutes. When the timer beeps, do a natural pressure release for about 10 minutes, then quick release any remaining pressure.

5. Carefully open the lid and transfer the drumstick to a baking sheet. Broil the drumsticks until golden brown for about 3-5 minutes.

6. Sprinkle with more cilantro and serve hot.

Pizza Pull Apart Bread

Preparation time: 10 minutes

Cook time: 10 minutes

Total time: 20 minutes

Ingredients:

- 2 cans of pizza dough
- 1/3 cup of olive oil
- 2 cups of mozzarella cheese
- 2 tbsp. of fresh parsley, chopped
- 4 cloves garlic minced
- 1 pack mini pepperonis
- Pizza sauce for dipping

Cooking Instructions:

1. Cut the pizza dough with a pizza cutter into 1-inch strips, then about 1 to 2 inch sections.

2. In a medium bowl, combine together the ingredients. Use your hands to toss all ingredients. Add the mixture into either a spring form pan, or Bundt pan.

3. Pour 1 cup of water into the bottom of your Instant Pot and place the pan inside your pot.

4. Secure the lid in place and close the vent. Select Manual, High Pressure for 10 minutes.

5. When the timer beeps, do a quick pressure release. Carefully open the lid and allow to cool.

6. Serve and enjoy!

Cilantro Jalapeño Hummus

Preparation time: 10 minutes

Cook time: 25 minutes

Total time: 35 minutes

Makes: 2 cups

Ingredients:

- 1 cup of cooked/canned Chickpeas/Garbanzo Beans, rinsed and drained
- 1 tablespoon of Homemade Tahini
- ½ cup of cilantro, chopped-stems and all
- ¼ cup of Jalapeño Peppers, seeds removed
- 1 teaspoon of cumin
- 1 teaspoon of chopped onion
- ½ teaspoon of sea salt
- ½ cup pf avocado oil

Cooking Instructions:

1. Dump all of the ingredients to a food processor and blend until combined.

2. If you desired dried Garbanzo Beans— soak beans overnight in water. Rinse and drain.

3. Add the beans into the bottom of your Instant Pot. Cover the beans with homemade vegetable broth, water, or stock of choice.

4. Secure the lid in place and close the vent. Select Manual, High Pressure for 25 minutes.

5. When the timer beeps, do a quick pressure release. Carefully remove the lid and give everything a good stir.

6. Serve immediately and enjoy!

Artichoke & Spinach Dip Applebee's Copycat

Preparation time: 2 minutes

Cook time: 4 minutes

Total time: 6 minutes

Servings: 10

Calories: 330 kcal

Ingredients:

- 8 ounces of cream cheese
- 10 ounces of box Frozen spinach
- 16 ounces Shredded Parm cheese
- 8 ounces Shredded mozzarella
- ½ cup of chicken broth
- 14 ounces can artichoke hearts
- ½ cup of sour cream
- ½ cup of mayo
- 3 cloves garlic
- 1 teaspoon of onion powder

Cooking Instructions:

1. Add the 3 cloves garlic into the bottom of your Instant Pot and pour ½ cup of chicken broth.

2. Drain the Artichokes and add them into the pot. Add the Frozen spinach, sour cream, cream cheese, and mayo and onion powder.

3. Secure the lid in place and close the vent. Select Manual, High Pressure for 4 minutes.

4. When the timer beeps, do a quick pressure release. Carefully open the lid and stir in cheese. Transfer to a bowl to thicken as it cools.

5. Serve with corn chips or bread and enjoy!

Hawaiian Meatballs

Preparation time: 5 minutes

Cook time: 5 minutes

Total time: 10 minutes

Servings: 4

Ingredients:

- 1 package Cooked Perfect Sweet Italian meatballs
- 1 can pineapple chunks with juice
- 1 red pepper, chopped
- ¾ cup of brown sugar
- 1 tbsp. of soy sauce
- ¼ cup of red onion
- 1/3 cup of water

Cooking Instructions:

1. Add all the ingredients (except for corn starch) into the bottom of your Instant Pot and stir.

2. Secure the lid in place and ensure that the valve is in sealing position. Select Manual, High Pressure for 5 minutes.

3. When the timer beeps, do a natural pressure release for about 10 minutes, then quick release any remaining pressure. Carefully open the lid.

4. Press the Sauté function on your Instant Pot and whisk in 1 tablespoon of cornstarch until thickened.

5. Serve over rice and enjoy!

Bacon Cheeseburger Dip

Preparation time: 6 minutes

Cook time: 4 minutes

Total time: 10 minutes

Ingredients:

- ½ lb. of lean ground beef
- 4-5 slices of bacon cut into bite sized pieces
- 10 ounces can diced tomatoes with green chili peppers
- 8 ounces cream cheese cut into cubes
- 8 ounces shredded Cheddar-Monterey Jack cheese
- 4 tbsp. of water

Cooking Instructions:

1. Turn on the Instant Pot and press the Sauté function.

2. When hot, add the bacon pieces and cook until browned. Scoop out and place on plate lined with paper towel.

3. Add in ground beef and cook until no longer pink. Turn off your Instant Pot and drain off excess grease.

4. Add the bacon, water, diced tomatoes, and cream cheese back into the pot and do not stir. Secure the lid in place and close the vent.

5. Select Manual, High Pressure for 4 minutes. When the timer beeps, do a quick pressure release.

6. Carefully open the lid and stir in cheese. Continue stirring until everything is well combined.

7. Serve with tortilla chips and enjoy!

Sweet BBQ Meatballs

Yield: 42 meatballs

Preparation time: 5 minutes

Cook time: 5 minutes

Total time: 10 minutes

Ingredients:

- 1 bag (48 oz.) frozen fully cooked beef meatballs
- 18 oz. BBQ Sauce (We used Masterpiece Original)
- 18 oz. grape jelly

Cooking Instructions:

1. Pour 1 cup of water into the bottom of your Instant Pot and add a steamer basket.

2. Add the frozen meatballs. Secure the lid in place and close the vent. Select Manual, High Pressure for 5 minutes.

3. When the timer beeps, do a quick pressure release. Carefully open the lid and remove the steamer basket and meatballs.

4. Drain the cooking water and add BBQ sauce and grape jelly to pot. Press the Sauté function and cook, stirring frequently, until jelly is melted and the sauce is smooth.

5. Add the heated meatballs and give everything a good stir to combine. Press the Keep Warm function to keep warm setting until ready to serve.

6. Serve and enjoy!

Easy Bacon Hot Dog Bites

Preparation time: 5 minutes

Cook time: 5 minutes

Total time: 10 minutes

Ingredients:

- 1 Pack Ball Park Hot Dogs
- ½ Jar of grape jelly
- ½ bottle of cocktail sauce
- 4 slices of Wright Brand Hickory Smoked Bacon

Cooking Instructions:

1. Cut up the bacon and hot dogs. Set the hot dogs aside.

2. Press the Sauté function on your Instant Pot and cook bacon until done. Separate the grease from the bacon using a colander.

3. Add the bacon and hot dogs back into the pot. Add the jelly and cocktail sauce and sauté, stirring until the jelly is liquid.

4. Secure the lid in place and close the vent. Select Manual, High Pressure for 5 minutes. When the timer beeps, do a quick pressure release.

5. Carefully open the lid and transfer to a serving dish to thicken as the sauce cools.

6. Serve and enjoy!

DESSERTS

Chocolate Pots De Crème

Yield: 6

Preparation time: 10 minutes

Cook time: 6 minutes

Total time: 16 minutes

Ingredients:

- 1 ½ cups of heavy cream
- ½ cup of whole milk
- 5 large egg yolks
- ¼ cup of sugar
- Pinch of salt
- 8 oz. bittersweet chocolate, melted
- Whipped cream and grated chocolate for decoration, optional

Cooking Instructions:

1. In a medium saucepan, add the cream and milk to a simmer.

2. In a medium bowl, whisk together the egg yolks, sugar, and salt. Whisk in the hot cream and milk. Whisk in chocolate until blended.

3. Add the mixture into 6 custard cups. Pour 1 ½ cups of water into the bottom of your Instant Pot and place the trivet.

4. Add 3 cups on the trivet and place a second trivet on top of the cups. Stack the remaining 3 cups on top of the second trivet.

5. Secure the lid in place and close the vent. Select Manual, High Pressure for 6 minutes.

6. When the timer beeps, do a natural pressure release for about 10 minutes, then quick release any remaining pressure.

7. Carefully open the lid and remove the cups to a wire rack to cool uncovered. When cool, refrigerate covered with plastic wrap for at least 4 hours or overnight.

8. Serve and enjoy!

Pumpkin Banana Chocolate Chip Bundt Cake

Preparation time: 12 minutes

Cook time: 45 minutes

Total time: 57 minutes

Servings: 12

Ingredients:

- ¾ cup of whole wheat flour
- ¾ cup of unbleached all-purpose flour
- ½ tsp. of salt
- 1 tsp. of baking soda
- ½ tsp. of baking powder
- ¾ tsp. of pumpkin pie spice
- ¾ cup of sugar
- 1 medium banana mashed
- 2 tbsp. of canola oil
- ½ cup of 2% Greek yogurt
- 1/2 15 oz. can 100% pureed pumpkin. We used homemade puree measured on a food scale. 7.5 oz.
- 1 egg
- ½ tsp. of pure vanilla extract
- 2/3 cup of semi-sweet chocolate chips or chocolate chunks

Cooking Instructions:

1. In a medium bowl, combine together the flour, salt, baking soda, baking powder, pumpkin pie spice and reserve aside.

2. In a separate bowl, combine together the sugar, banana, oil, yogurt, pureed pumpkin, egg and vanilla with an electric mixer.

3. Gradually add the dry ingredients with the mixer on low until incorporated. Fold in the chocolate chips.

4. Grease the Bundt pan and add the batter to the Bundt pan. Cover the pan with paper towels and then foil. Pour 1.5 cups of water into the bottom of your Instant Pot.

5. Place the Bundt pan on top. Secure the lid in place and close the vent. Select Manual, High Pressure for 35 minutes.

6. When the timer beeps, do a natural pressure release for about 10 minutes, then quick release any remaining pressure.

7. Carefully open the lid and remove the Bundt pan. Allow the pan to cool for a couple of minutes before opening it.

8. Serve and enjoy!

Apple Crisp

Servings: 3-4

Preparation time: 5 minutes

Cook time: 8 minutes

Total time: 13 minutes

Ingredients:

- 5 medium sized apples, peeled and chopped into chunks
- 2 teaspoons of cinnamon
- ½ teaspoon of nutmeg
- ½ cup of water
- 1 tablespoon of maple syrup
- 4 tablespoons of butter
- ¾ cup of old fashioned rolled oats
- ¼ cup of flour
- ¼ cup of brown sugar
- ½ teaspoon of salt

Cooking Instructions:

1. Add the apples into the bottom of your Instant Pot.

2. Sprinkle with cinnamon and nutmeg. Top with water and maple syrup.

3. Add the butter to melt. In a medium bowl, mix together the melted butter, oats, flour, brown sugar and salt. Drop by the spoonful on top of the apples.

4. Secure the lid in place and close the vent. Select Manual, High Pressure for 8 minutes.

5. When the timer beeps, do a natural pressure release for about 15 minutes. Carefully open the lid and allow to sit for a couple of minutes to thicken the sauce.

6. Serve warm and top with vanilla ice cream.

Molten Brownie Pudding

Preparation time: 10 minutes

Cook time: 30 minutes

Total time: 40 minutes

Ingredients:

- 1 ½ cups of water
- 7 tbsp. of butter, melted & divided
- 1 cup of sugar
- 2 eggs
- ¼ cup of flour
- ¼ cup plus 2 tbsp. of unsweetened cocoa powder
- 1 tsp. of vanilla
- 1/8 tsp. of salt
- ¼ cup of semisweet chocolate chips
- ¼ cup of milk chocolate chips

Cooking Instructions:

1. Add the 1 ½ cups of water into the bottom of your Instant Pot and place the steam rack inside.

2. Butter a 6- to 7-inch soufflé or baking dish with 1 tbsp. of the butter. In a medium bowl, use an electric hand mixer to beat the sugar and eggs until light and fluffy, for about 4 to 5 minutes.

3. In a separate bowl, whisk together the flour, cocoa and salt. Add the mixture to the sugar and egg mixture and give everything a good mix to combine.

4. Mix in the vanilla and the rest of the 6 tbsp. of melted butter and give everything a good mix to combine. Add the mixture into the prepared dish and sprinkle with the chocolate chips.

5. Place the dish on the steam rack and add into your Instant Pot. Secure the lid in place and close the vent. Select Manual, High Pressure for 30 minutes.

6. When the timer beeps, do a quick pressure release. Carefully open the lid sand remove the baking dish with tongs. Allow to cool for about 5 minutes before serving.

7. Serve with a scoop of vanilla ice cream, if desired.

French Apple Cobbler

Preparation time: 25 minutes

Cook time: 35 minutes

Total time: 1 hour

Servings: 4 - 6

Calories: 225 kcal

Ingredients:

Apple Mixture:

- 4 cups of sliced apples
- ½ cup of coconut sugar
- 2 tablespoons of gluten free flour
- ½ teaspoon of cinnamon
- ¼ teaspoon of nutmeg
- ½ teaspoon of sea salt
- 1 teaspoon of vanilla
- ¼ cup of water

Cobbler:

- ¾ cup of gluten free flour
- ¼ cup of coconut sugar
- 1 teaspoon of sea salt
- ½ teaspoon of baking powder
- ½ teaspoon of baking soda
- 4 ounces of applesauce

Cooking Instructions:

1. In a medium bowl, mix all the apple ingredients.

2. In a separate bowl, mix all the ingredients for cobbler topping. Spoon the cobbler mix on top of apple mixture. Add the bowl containing the mixture in your rack.

3. Pour 1 cup of water into the bottom of your Instant Pot. Add the bowl on rack and place into the pot. Secure the lid in place and close the vent.

4. Select Manual, High Pressure for 25 minutes. When the timer beeps, do a natural pressure release for about 10 minutes.

5. Carefully open the lid and remove the bowl and rack. Place the bowl under your broiler and broil until your desired crisp is achieved for about 5 minutes.

6. Serve and enjoy!

Bourbon Sticky Toffee Pudding

Preparation time: 15 minutes

Cook time: 25 minutes

Total time: 40 minutes

Servings: 4

Calories: 242 kcal

Ingredients:

- ½ cup of chopped dates
- ½ tsp. of baking soda
- 6 tbsp. of hot water
- 2 tbsp. of good quality bourbon
- 3 tbsp. of unsalted butter
- 2 tbsp. of Milk
- 2/3 cup of flour
- 1 tsp. of baking powder
- 1 egg
- ½ tsp. of cinnamon
- 1/8 tsp. of cloves
- 1/8 tsp. of Allspice
- ¼ tsp. of salt
- ½ cup store bought salted caramel sauce

Cooking Instructions:

1. In a medium bowl, add the bourbon, hot water and baking soda and stir to combine.

2. Chop the dates into ½ inch pieces. In a microwave safe bowl, combine together milk and butter. Microwave on low for about 3 to 4 minutes to melt the butter.

3. Remove bowl from the microwave and add the flour. Add the spices, baking powder and salt and give everything a good stir to combine.

4. In a separate bowl, beat the egg and add to the flour mixture. Add the dates and water mixture. Stir all the ingredients together.

5. Spray 4 ramekins with non-stick spray. Divide the mixture evenly between the 4 ramekins. Spray 4 small pieces of foil with non-stick cooking spray and cover the ramekins with foil.

6. Add in the wire rack and place the ramekins on the wire rack. Add into the bottom of your Instant Pot. Add 4 cups of hot water into the Instant Pot.

7. Secure the lid in place and close the vent. Press the Steam function to cook for 25 minutes. When the timer beeps, do a natural pressure release for about 15 minutes.

8. Carefully open the lid and remove foil. Run a thin knife around the ramekins and turn out puddings on small dessert plates. Drizzle with caramel sauce.

9. Serve and enjoy!

Apple Cinnamon Cake

Preparation time: 15 minutes

Cook time: 1 hour

Total time: 1 hour 15 minutes

Servings: 8

Calories: 275 kcal

Ingredients:

- 3 cups of apples (cored, peeled and diced)
- ½ tbsp. of ground cinnamon
- 2 tbsp. of sugar
- 1 ½ cups flour (one and a half cup)
- ½ tbsp. of baking powder
- ½ tsp. of sea salt
- ½ cup of vegetable oil
- ¾ cup of sugar
- 2 tbsp. of orange juice
- 1 tsp. of vanilla extract
- 2 large eggs at room temperature
- Powdered sugar for sprinkling on top

Water Bath for the Cake:

- 1 cup of water

Cooking Instructions:

1. Grease a 7" cake pan. Add the chopped apple slices with cinnamon and 2 tbsp. of sugar and reserve aside.

2. In a medium bowl, mix together the dry ingredients: flour, baking powder and salt together and reserve aside.

3. In another bowl, whisk wet ingredients: oil, orange juice, sugar, vanilla and eggs. Add the wet ingredients into the dry ingredients and mix well.

4. Pour half of batter in the cake pan. Spread half of apples on top of the batter. Add the rest of the batter covering most of the apple pieces.

5. Spread the rest of the half apples and any juices on top. Cover the cake pan tightly with aluminum foil.

6. Pour 1 cup of water into the bottom of your Instant Pot. Add the cake pan on the trivet and place in your pot. Secure the lid in place and close the vent.

7. Select Manual, High Pressure for 60 minutes. When the timer beeps, do a natural pressure release for about 10 minutes.

8. Carefully open the lid and remove the trivet. Remove the aluminum foil and let to cool. Sprinkle with powdered sugar.

9. Serve warm with a bowl of vanilla ice cream!

Mini-Lemon Cheesecakes

Serves: 6

Preparation time: 10 minutes

Cook time: 8 minutes

Total time: 18 minutes

Ingredients:

- 6 half pint mason jars
- 16 ounces of cream cheese, room temp
- ½ cup of sugar
- 1 teaspoon of flour
- ½ teaspoon of vanilla
- ¼ cup of sour cream, room temp
- 1 tablespoon of lemon juice
- Zest of 1 lemon
- 3 eggs, room temp
- 1 jar lemon curd (found in the jam & jelly aisle)
- Raspberries (optional)
- 1.5 cups of water

Cooking Instructions:

1. In a medium bowl, beat together the cream cheese, sugar, and flour until mixture is creamy with no lumps.

2. Beat in vanilla, sour cream, lemon juice, and lemon zest just until mixed well. Beat in one egg at a time just until mixed. Fill each jar with ¼ cup of cheesecake batter.

3. Add 1 tablespoon of lemon curd on top of batter. Add another ¼ cup of cheesecake batter to each jar on top of the lemon curd. Loosely cover each jar with a piece aluminum foil.

4. Pour 1.5 cups of water into the bottom of your Instant Pot and place the trivet. Place the 3 jars on top of the trivet. Stack the other 3 jars on the first three.

5. Secure the lid in place and close the vent. Select Manual, High Pressure for 8 minutes. When the timer beeps, do a natural pressure release for about 10 minutes.

6. Carefully open the lid and remove the jars. Allow to and garnish with additional lemon curd and raspberries.

7. Serve immediately and enjoy!

www.ingramcontent.com/pod-product-compliance
Lightning Source LLC
Chambersburg PA
CBHW081748100526
44592CB00015B/2339